Living and Working in the UK

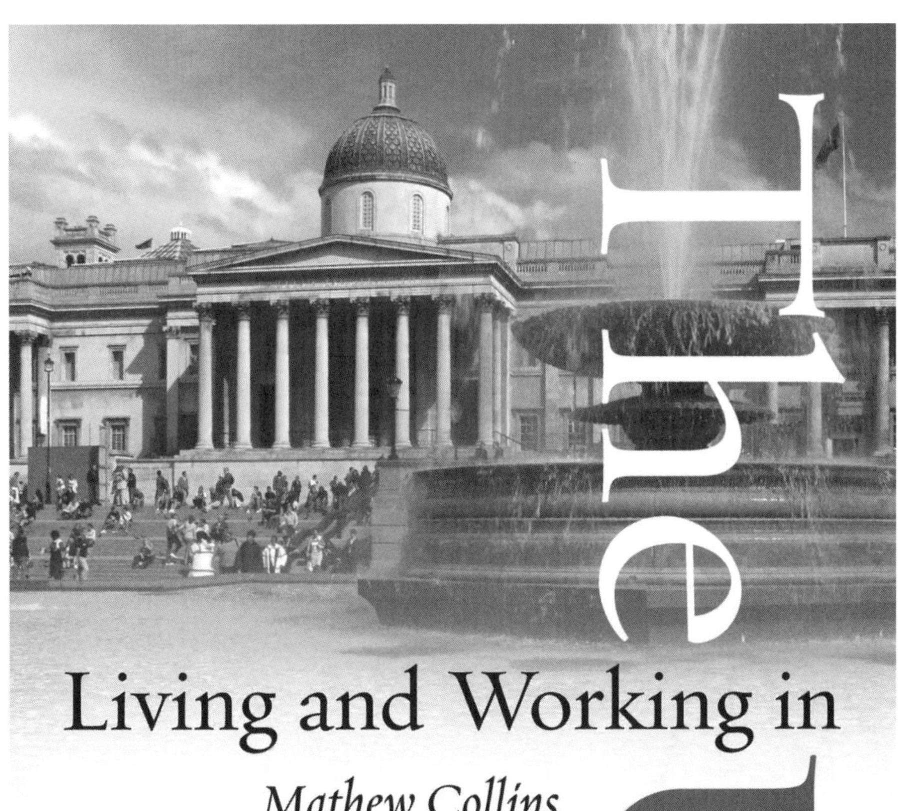

Living and Working in The UK

Mathew Collins
& Nicky Barclay

'An indispensible read for anyone thinking of Living and Working in Britain.'

A PRACTICAL GUIDE

howtobooks

Published by How To Books Ltd,
Spring Hill House, Spring Hill Road
Begbroke, Oxford OX5 1RX
Tel: (01865) 375794. Fax: (01865) 379162
email: info@howtobooks.co.uk
http://www.howtobooks.co.uk

British Library Cataloguing in Publication Data
A catalogue record for this book is available from the British Library

ISBN 13: 978-1-84528-067-3
ISBN 10: 1-84528-067-9

Cover design by Baseline Arts, Oxford
Produced for How To Books by Deer Park Productions, Tavistock, Devon
Typeset by PDQ Typesetting, Newcastle-under-Lyme, Staffs.
Printed and bound by Bell & Bain, Glasgow

Contents

Preface

Managed Migration, Entry Clearance, Life in the UK Test, OISC (Office of the Immigration Services Commission), Registered Education Providers, BAC (British Accreditation Council), Further Leave to Remain, Selective Admission, Making Migration Work for Britain are all terms within the UK immigration industry. What do these mean and where can one start to understand the complex nature of how immigration rules, policy and procedures have evolved over the years?

If you are an overseas national wanting to spend time in the United Kingdom you will have some form of experience with the United Kingdom immigration authorities. This may be before departure to the UK by way of an Entry Clearance Application, on arrival in the UK at a port of entry or an application for Indefinite Leave to Remain once you have entered the country. For the unlucky this may be during departure, forced or voluntarily.

Immigration is now more complex than ever. When you relocate from one country to another you are in a vulnerable position. You need to adapt quickly to a new culture. Not only that, but many customs and behaviours can be very different. You may have many questions but don't know who to ask for the answers.

My colleague and co-author, Nicky Barclay and I deal with immigration applications and relocating people every day. In today's world more people than ever move for the purposes of family, employment, and business. Usually these people are information hungry and want to know as much as they can about their new destination and how to carry on with their lives in a law-abiding fashion once they get there.

If you want to stay permanently you may also need to know about the history of this country and numerous other subject materials to sit the newly introduced 'Life in the UK' citizenship test.

This book has been designed to help people who are foreign nationals who are in the United Kingdom or those thinking of coming.

Part One provides an introduction to, and background and history of, the United Kingdom, including information you need to know before sitting the citizenship test.

Part Two covers the most common categories under the immigration rules and policy. This includes existing criteria, supporting documents needed to make an application, and the forms you need and how to apply.

Part Three gives a comprehensive account of things you need to know on topics such as housing, the education system, healthcare, taxes, banking and lots of other useful information and contacts.

Every applicant will have different personal circumstances and assessing yourself against the current criteria of a particular category and understanding how a Case Officer may interpret the policy and procedures can be confusing. Where you are unsure, you should always take advice from an OISC Registered Immigration Practitioner.

We have used our knowledge and experience as Registered Immigration and Relocation Practitioners to put together this book to help you.

The book is also an ideal tool for personnel departments to provide to new foreign national employees and to assist them in their induction.

If you want to enter under any other category and are intending to live in the UK, or you are in the UK and want to extend your visa or apply for citizenship, you will find information, advice and contact details that you will need to help you.

Completing this book against a backdrop of ever-changing rules and regulations has been a challenge. Alongside managing a busy practice and the day-to-day demands of our clients we very much appreciate the assistance of Kim Bailey who has assisted in getting this book to print. Her dedication and application to the research, writing and organisation of this project has been invaluable.

After reading this book we hope you find the information you are looking for. It will certainly be one of the best starting points you will find. If you still have questions you can contact us at our office in London.

Good Reading and Good Luck!

Mathew Collins and Nicky Barclay

PART ONE

1

United Kingdom past and present

UK OR BRITAIN?

The full title of the country is the United Kingdom of Great Britain and Northern Ireland. The UK is made up of four nations: England, Scotland, Wales and Northern Ireland. However, a lot of people say 'Great Britain' or 'Britain'. In general, Britain refers to the mainland and Great Britain includes Northern Ireland, the Channel Islands and the Isle of Man.

The people who live in the four nations are all British. The individual differences and culture within each are still greatly treasured, particularly in sporting competitions, with the English, Welsh, Scottish and Irish people still retaining their competitiveness and pride in their own nation.

BRITAIN'S OVERSEAS TERRITORIES AND CROWN DEPENDENCIES

Britain has 14 Overseas Territories, spread throughout the globe. They range from the tiny island of Pitcairn, with its 47 inhabitants, set in the middle of the Pacific Ocean, to Bermuda, which has a population of 62,059 and is one of the world's major financial centres.

The Overseas Territories are: Anguilla, British Antarctic Territory, Bermuda, British Indian Ocean Territory, British Virgin Islands, Cayman Islands, Falkland Islands, Gibraltar, Montserrat, St Helena and Dependencies (Ascension Island and Tristan da Cunha), Turk and Caicos Islands, Pitcairn Island, South Georgia and South Sandwich Islands, Sovereign Base Areas on Cyprus.

The Crown Dependencies are not part of the United Kingdom but are internally self-governing dependencies of the Crown. The Crown Dependencies are the Isle of Man, the Bailiwick of Jersey and the Bailiwick of Guernsey.

LIVING IN THE UK

The UK is an exciting, eclectic, successful and progressive place to live and work in the 21st century.

With a population approaching nearly 60 million, the UK is a growing country, offering a wealth of opportunities to people of all ages, backgrounds and cultures from across the world. Consequently, becoming a UK citizen is a much prized possession.

The UK – different countries offering different things

The UK is made up of four nations or countries.

England

England is a country of great contrast and diversity, both in the places you can go to and in the people you meet. All the regions of England are within easy reach of the exciting capital city, London, famed for first-class culture, fascinating history and pageantry, its world-class restaurants and theatres.

Scotland

Scotland is everything you imagine – whisky, golf, romance of the clans and a wealth of castles and historic sites. The Highlands area is one of the last wildernesses in Europe.

Wales

Wales captivates visitors with its rich character and landscapes. The Welsh speak their own Celtic language as well as English and have their own culture, poetry and song, which they celebrate in concerts and unique summer festivals known as *eisteddfodau*.

Northern Ireland

Northern Ireland is known for its vibrant cities with shopping, nightlife and festivals, outdoor activities, fabulous food and unspoilt retreats where you can unwind, relax and recharge.

KEY FACTS AND FIGURES

- The mid-2004 population of the constituent countries of the United Kingdom is estimated as follows:

Sources: Mid-year population estimates 2004: Office for National Statistics, General Register Office for Scotland Northern Ireland Statistics and Research Agency.

	Population	Per cent of total UK population
ENGLAND	50,093,800	83.7
WALES	2,952,500	*4.9*
SCOTLAND	5,078,400	*8.5*
NORTHERN IRELAND	1,710,300	*2.9*
UNITED KINGDOM	59,834,900	

- The native-born English outnumber their Scots and Welsh counterparts by nine to one.
- A census of the population has taken place every 10 years since 1801. The next census is due in 2011.
- Total net worth of the UK including financial assets at the end of 2004 was £5,843 billion, an increase of £404 billion on the previous year.
- Currency is (£) pound sterling or GBP (Great British Pound).

- The unemployment rate in 2005 was 4.7 per cent.
- The number of unemployed people was 1.42 million in 2005.
- The economy is one of the strongest in Europe; inflation, interest rates, and unemployment remain low.
- Inflation rate 1.4 per cent.
- Most people work between 31 and 45 hours per week.
- 7.5 per cent of people living in Britain were born abroad.
- 51 per cent of the population is made up of women and they make up 45 per cent of the workforce.
- The UK is one of the quartet of trillion-dollar economies of Western Europe.
- The United Kingdom has 23 cultural and natural heritage sites listed by UNESCO.

For more specific facts and figures, the UK government's website for the Office for National Statistics, which brings together in one place a wide range of demographic, social, industrial and economic statistics, can be found at http://www.statistics.gov.uk/.

THE UK'S CAPITAL

The capital of the UK is London, one of the great cities in the world. It has an unrivalled cultural and artistic heritage, helping to confirm its place as a vibrant and dynamic city.

London is one of the few global centres for international business and is comparable in size to many national economies. It is certainly one of the largest cities in the developed world in terms of its built-up area, and is the most populous city in the European Union, of which the UK is a member. London is home to over 7 million people and has a resident workforce of some 3.4 million, which is supplemented further by a large number of commuters. It is also one of the European Union's most densely settled areas: only Copenhagen, Brussels and Paris are more densely populated.

The service sector dominates London's economy. Key services among the sector are finance and business services, the public sector, tourism and hospitality and the creative and cultural industries. Finance and business services alone accounted for 35 per cent of London's Gross Value Added (GVA) in 1998. However, manufacturing is still an important part of London's economy, accounting for over 11 per cent of London's GVA in 1998 and the third highest region in cash terms, with GVA of £13 billion.

Over 300 languages are spoken and the UK government's 2001 Census shows that 29 per cent of London's population belonged to a minority ethnic group. One in five small businesses are owned or managed by members of minority ethnic communities.

BRIEF HISTORY OF BRITAIN

Knowledge of Britain before the Roman Conquest, which began in AD 43, is based mainly on archeological research. It was only after the Saxon settlements in the 5th century AD that Britain really emerges into the history books.

Certainly Britain is one of the most ancient and historically wealthy countries in the world. Its history is difficult to summarise in a few pages, but it has definitely had a bloody and unsettled past.

From the many invasions of England, with the Anglo Saxon (Germanic) occupation and the Norman Conquest in 1066 and the Battle of Hastings, through to the major wars of the 20th century:

the First World War (1914–18) and the Second World War 1939–1945 to 21st century battles in Iraq, Britain has been a fighting and persuasive power.

Roman Conquest

The Romans began to expand into Britain some decades after Julius Caesar had made an exploratory push into Britain in 55 BC. It was the following century when they returned to conquer and control the island (except Wales and the North). Strong opposition from the inhabitants resulted in the Emperor Hadrian building a wall across the narrow neck of land between the North Sea and Irish Channel. Large parts of Hadrian's Wall are still there today. The division he created eventually established the kingdom of Scotland.

The Romans had a lasting effect on the island, building roads, creating law, and words from their own Latin language which are still used in English today.

Norman Conquest

In the 8th and 9th centuries, Vikings from what are now Denmark and Norway came to settle and farm, conquering most of the east of England and the northeast of Scotland.

When William, Duke of Normandy, sailed from France in dispute over the inheritance of the crown, he landed on the south coast of England and defeated King Harold of England in 1066 at the Battle of Hastings.

The Middle Ages

This term is commonly used to cover the period between the Norman Conquest and around 1485, the beginning of the Tudor dynasty when Henry VII came to the throne of England. During this time the English monarchy strove to dominate the Scots, the Welsh, the Irish and to pursue dynastic and territorial ambitions in France.

Key documents

The National Archives, the British Library and the Parliamentary Archives hold the key documents relating to UK history. Below are some examples of some of the more important documents in the UK's history.

Magna Carta

Magna Carta is often thought of as the cornerstone of liberty and the chief defence against arbitrary and unjust rule in England. In fact it contains few sweeping statements of principle, but is a series of concessions wrung from the unwilling King John by his rebellious barons in 1215. However, Magna Carta established for the first time a very significant constitutional principle, namely that the power of the king could be limited by a written grant.

Four copies of this original grant survive. Two are held at the British Library while the others can be seen in the cathedral archives at Lincoln and Salisbury.

Bills of Rights 1689

After the short-lived constitutional experiments that followed the Civil War, the supremacy of Parliament was finally enshrined in the Bill of Rights passed in December 1689.

Union with Scotland 1707

In the 16th century, legislation had united England and Wales. In 1707 Acts of Union were passed by the Parliaments of England and Scotland, forming the United Kingdom of Great Britain. These Acts abolished the Scottish Parliament and transferred the Scottish representatives to Westminster.

Rights to vote

In early 19th-century Britain very few people had the right to vote. The Reform Act of 1832 gave the vote in towns only to men who occupied property with an annual value of £10. Universal suffrage, with voting rights for women (though not for those under 30), did not arrive in Britain until February 1918. It wasn't until 1928 that women received the same voting rights at the same age as men.

With probably the best depth and breadth of recorded history anywhere in the world, a number of websites are now available which show and explain in detail the historical events and documents pertaining to Britain's past.

The British National Archives has an excellent website that explores what it has meant to be a citizen throughout a millennium of British history. It presents a selection of fascinating documents from the National Archives and Parliamentary Archives, many of them made available online for the first time. Each document is explained and set in its historical context, providing a unique insight into the past as seen through the records of the time. http://www.nationalarchives.gov.uk/pathways/citizenship/

Records of the UK government from Domesday to the present are available from the National Archives of England, Wales and the United Kingdom. It has one of the largest archival collections in the world, spanning 1,000 years of British history, from the Domesday Book of 1086 to government papers recently released to the public. http://www.nationalarchives.gov.uk/

OVERVIEW AND HISTORY OF THE MONARCHY

The monarchy is the oldest institution of government. The Queen's full title in the UK is 'Elizabeth the Second, by the Grace of God of the United Kingdom of Great Britain and Northern Ireland and of Her other Realms and Territories Queen, Head of the Commonwealth, Defender of the Faith'. Or in brief, she is known as Queen Elizabeth II. In the Channel Islands and the Isle of Man she is represented by a Lieutenant-Governor.

In addition to being Queen of the United Kingdom, the Queen is also head of state of 15 other realms and is Head of the Commonwealth. In each country where she is head of state, she is represented by a Governor-General, appointed by her on the advice of the ministers of the country concerned and independent of the UK government.

In the Overseas Territories, the Queen is usually represented by governors responsible to the UK government for the administration of the countries in which they serve.

The title to the Crown derives partly from statute and partly from common law rules of descent. Despite interruptions in the direct line of succession, inheritance has always been the way royal power has passed down the generations, with sons of the sovereign coming before daughters in succeeding to the throne. When a daughter does succeed, she becomes Queen Regnant and has the same powers as a King. The 'consort' of a king takes her husband's rank and style, becoming Queen. No special rank or privileges are given to the husband of a Queen Regnant.

Under the Act of Settlement of 1700, only Protestant descendants of Princess Sophia, the Electress of Hanover (a granddaughter of James I of England and VI of Scotland), are eligible to succeed. The order of succession to the throne can be altered only by common consent of the countries of the Commonwealth, of which the monarch is sovereign.

The sovereign succeeds to the throne as soon as his or her predecessor dies. He or she is at once proclaimed at an Accession Council, to which all members of the Privy Council are called. Members of the House of Lords, the Lord Mayor, Aldermen and other leading citizens of the City of London are also invited.

The coronation follows the accession. The ceremony takes place at Westminster Abbey in London in the presence of representatives of both houses of Parliament and all the major public organisations in the UK. The prime ministers and leading members of the Commonwealth nations and representatives of other countries also attend.

Origins of Parliament

Medieval Kings had to meet all royal expenses, private and public, out of their own income. If extra resources were needed for an emergency, such as going to war, the sovereign would seek help from his barons in the Great Council – a gathering of leading men who met several times a year.

During the 13th century, several English Kings found their own private revenue, together with aid from the barons, insufficient to meet the expenses of government. They therefore also called on representatives of counties, cities and towns to agree to additional taxation.

In time the Great Council came to include those who were summoned by name (who, broadly speaking, were later to form the House of Lords) and those who were representatives of communities – the Commons. These two groups, together with the sovereign, became known as 'Parliament' – a term meaning a meeting for parley or discussion.

Originally the sovereign's legislation needed only the agreement of his or her councillors. Later, starting with the right of individuals to present petitions, the Commons was eventually allowed to appeal to the Crown on behalf of groups of people.

In the 14th century, under King Edward III, it was accepted that there should be no taxation without parliamentary consent, still a fundamental principle today. In the 15th century, the Commons gained equal law-making powers with the Lords.

In the 17th century, tensions increased between Parliament and monarch, such that in 1641 the King and Parliament could not agree on the control of troops for repression of the Irish Rebellion. Civil war broke out the following year, leading to the execution of King Charles I in January 1649.

Following the restoration of the monarchy in 1660, the role of Parliament was enhanced by the events of 1688–89 (the 'Glorious Revolution') and the passage of the Bill of Rights which established the authority of Parliament over the King, and enshrined in law the principle of freedom of speech in parliamentary debates.

The year 1707 brought the Union of England with Scotland and the first Parliament of Great Britain. Growing pressure for reform of

Parliament in the 18th and 19th centuries led to a series of Reform Acts which extended the vote to most men over 21 in 1867 and, finally, to women over 21 in 1928.

The legislative primacy of the House of Commons over the Lords was confirmed in the 20th century by the passing of the Parliament Acts of 1911 and 1949.

Today proceedings in Parliament are broadcast on digital television, as well as recorded in official reports.

The Privy Council

The Privy Council was formerly the chief source of executive power in the state, but as the system of Cabinet government developed in the 18th century, the Cabinet took on much of its role.

Today, the Privy Council is the main way in which ministers advise the Queen on the approval of Orders in Council, such as those granting Royal Charters or enacting subordinate legislation, or on the issue of royal proclamations such as the summoning or dissolving of Parliament.

There are about 500 Privy Councillors, whose appointments are for life. The Privy Council consists of all members of the Cabinet, other senior politicians, senior judges and some individuals from the Commonwealth. Only members of the government of the day, however, play any part in its policy work. The Prime Minister recommends new members of the Privy Council to the Sovereign.

There are a number of Privy Council committees, of which the Cabinet is technically one, normally comprising ministers with the relevant policy interest, such as those dealing with legislation from the Channel Islands and the Isle of Man. Except for the Judicial Committee, membership is confined to members of the administration of the day.

The Judicial Committee of the Privy Council is the final court of appeal from courts in UK Overseas Territories and those Commonwealth countries which decided to keep this method of appeal after their independence. In addition, the Committee hears appeals from the Channel Islands and the Isle of Man. It is the court of final appeal for determining devolution issues, that is, issues as to the limits of the powers and functions of the executive and legislative authorities in Scotland, Northern Ireland and Wales.

It also has a limited jurisdiction to hear certain ecclesiastical appeals. Members of the Judicial Committee include the Secretary of State for Constitutional Affairs and Lord Chancellor, the Lords of Appeal in Ordinary, other Privy Councillors who hold or have held high judicial office and certain judges from the Commonwealth.

OVERVIEW OF UK GOVERNMENT

The United Kingdom is a parliamentary democracy. It is also a constitutional monarchy in which ministers of the Crown govern in the name of the sovereign, who is both head of state and head of the government.

There is no 'written constitution' in the UK. Instead, the relationship between the state and the people relies on statute law, common law and conventions.

The UK Parliament makes primary legislation – other than for matters devolved to the Scottish Parliament and the Northern Ireland Assembly – and is the highest authority in the land. It continues to have the supreme authority for government and law-making in the UK as a whole.

The executive comprises the government (members of the Cabinet and other ministers responsible for policies), government departments and agencies, local authorities, public corporations, independent regulatory bodies and certain other organisations subject to ministerial control. The judiciary determines common law and interprets statutes.

In her role as monarch, the Queen is head of the executive and plays an integral part in the legislature. She heads the judiciary and is both the commander-in-chief of all the armed forces of the Crown and supreme governor of the established Church of England.

Overview of Devolution in Scotland, Wales and Northern Ireland

Following devolution, the responsibilities of the government's Secretaries of State for Scotland, Wales and Northern Ireland changed considerably, although they retain their positions in the UK Cabinet. They ensure that the reserved interests of the countries they represent are properly considered in central government and they lead the presentation of government policy in their parts of the UK. They are also responsible for safeguarding and promoting the devolution settlements of their respective countries.

The monarchy and government

As a result of a long process of change during which the monarchy's absolute power has been gradually reduced, custom now dictates that the Queen follows ministerial advice from her Prime Minister.

Within this framework she performs a range of important duties, such as summoning, proroguing (discontinue a session, parliament, for example) and dissolving Parliament and giving Royal Assent to legislation passed by the UK Parliament, the Scottish Parliament or the Northern Ireland Assembly.

The Queen formally appoints important office holders, including the Prime Minister and other government ministers, judges, officers in the armed forces, governors, diplomats, bishops and some other senior clergy of the Church of England.

In instances where people have been wrongly convicted of crimes, she is involved in pardoning them. She also bestows peerages, knighthoods and other honours on citizens every year.

In international affairs the Queen, as head of state, has the power to declare war and make peace, to recognise foreign states, to conclude treaties and to take over or give up territory.

The Queen holds Privy Council meetings, gives audiences to her ministers and officials in the UK and overseas, receives accounts of Cabinet decisions, reads dispatches and signs state papers. She is consulted on many aspects of national life and must show complete impartiality in the advice she gives.

The law states that a regent has to be appointed to perform the royal functions if the monarch is totally incapacitated. The regency follows the line of succession, provided that the person concerned has reached the age of 18. The first eight members of the Royal Family in order of succession to the Throne are: the Prince of Wales, Prince William of Wales, Prince Henry of Wales, the Duke of York, Princess Beatrice of York, Princess Eugenie of York, the Earl of Wessex, Lady Louise (daughter of the Earl of Wessex), and the Princess Royal.

What Parliament does

The main functions of Parliament are to pass laws, to provide – by voting for taxation – the means of carrying out the work of government, to scrutinise Government policy and administration, including proposals for expenditure, and to debate the major issues of the day. In the course of performing these tasks, Parliament brings the relevant facts and issues to the attention of the electorate.

It is also customary for Parliament to be informed before important international treaties and agreements are finalised and agreed. The making of treaties is, however, a royal prerogative carried out on the advice of the government and, strictly speaking, does not need parliamentary approval.

ABOUT POLITICAL PARTIES

The party system, which has existed since the 18th century, depends upon there being organised political groups, each of which presents its policies to the electorate for approval. Most candidates in elections, and almost all winning candidates, belong to one of the main parties.

Since the 1920s, Britain has had a predominantly two-party system. Since 1945, either the Conservative Party, whose origins go back to the 18th century, or the Labour Party, which emerged in the last decade of the 19th century, has held power. The Liberal Democrats were formed in 1988 when the Liberal Party, which also traces its origins to the 18th century, merged with the Social Democratic Party, which was founded in 1981.

Other parties include two national parties, Plaid Cymru, the Party of Wales (founded in 1925), and the Scottish National Party (founded in 1934). Northern Ireland has a number of parties. They include the Ulster Unionists, formed in the early part of the 20th century, the Democratic Unionists, founded in 1971 by a group that broke away from the Ulster Unionists, the Social Democratic and Labour Party, founded in 1970, and Sinn Féin.

All those elected to Parliament and who serve their local community or constituency are paid a salary and can claim expenses. They all use the initials MP (Member of Parliament) after their names to show they are in public office. MPs are elected from 659 constituencies.

The party that wins most seats (although not necessarily the most votes) at a general election, or which has the support of a majority of members in the House of Commons, usually becomes the government. By tradition, the sovereign invites the leader of that party to form a government.

About 100 members of the governing party in the House of Commons and the House of Lords receive ministerial appointments (including appointment to the Cabinet) on the advice of the Prime Minister. The largest minority party becomes the official opposition, with its own leader and 'shadow cabinet'.

Political parties in Parliament

Leaders of the current government and opposition sit opposite one another on the front benches in the debating chamber of the House of Commons. Their supporters, called the 'backbenchers', sit behind them. There are similar seating arrangements for the parties in the House of Lords but those peers who do not wish to be associated with any political party choose to sit on the 'crossbenches'.

The effectiveness of the party system in Parliament relies to a large extent on the relationship between the government and the opposition parties. Depending on the relative strengths of the parties in the House of Commons, the opposition may try to overthrow the government by defeating it on a 'matter of confidence' vote.

However, in general, the opposition aims to contribute to the formulation of policy and legislation by constructive criticism, by opposing government proposals with which it disagrees, by tabling amendments to government Bills, and by putting forward its own policies in order to improve its chances of winning the next general election.

The government Chief Whips in the Commons and the Lords, in consultation with their opposition counterparts, arrange the scheduling of government business. Collectively, the Chief Whips are often referred to as 'the usual channels' when the question of finding time for a particular item of business is being discussed.

The Chief Whips and their assistants, who are usually chosen by the party leaders, manage their parliamentary parties. Their duties include keeping members informed of forthcoming parliamentary business, maintaining the party's voting strength by ensuring members attend important debates, and passing on to the party leadership the opinions of backbench members.

Legislation in 2000 made party funding more open. It specifies that:

- parties can only accept donations of over £200 from 'permissible donors', who are individuals on the UK electoral register, registered companies incorporated in the EU which do business in the UK, registered political parties, or trade unions
- all donations of over £5,000 to a political party's central organisation must be reported to the Electoral Commission on a quarterly basis, or weekly during a general election campaign
- all donations of over £1,000 to accounting units, such as a constituency association, must be reported to the Electoral Commission
- individual MPs and other people elected to office, including MEPs, members of the devolved assemblies of Wales and Northern Ireland and the Scottish Parliament, members of local authorities and the Mayor of London, are subject to similar controls on the source of donations and have to report to the Electoral Commission any donations over £1,000
- political parties are subject to a cap on campaign spending applied before a General Election; a party has an allowance of £30,000 for each constituency contested
- third parties at elections, such as trade unions, are subject to expenditure limits set at 5 per cent of the maximum for political parties.

Who can vote?

To vote in parliamentary elections in the UK you must be a British citizen, a citizen of another Commonwealth country or of the Irish Republic, as well as being resident in the UK, aged 18 or over, included in the register of electors for the constituency and not subject to any legal incapacity to vote. The right to vote at 18 years was established in 1969. Previously the age to vote was 21 years and was set in 1928. To ensure your name is entered on the electoral register, visit www.electoralcommission.org.uk.

British citizens who live abroad can vote in the UK elections for up to 15 years after leaving.

People not entitled to vote include members of the House of Lords, foreign nationals resident in the UK (other than Commonwealth citizens or citizens of the Irish Republic), some patients detained under mental health legislation, sentenced prisoners and people convicted within the previous five years of corrupt or illegal election practices.

Members of the armed forces, Crown servants and staff of the British Council employed overseas (together with their wives or husbands if accompanying them) may be registered at an address in the constituency where they would be living if they were not serving abroad. British citizens living abroad may apply to register as electors for a period of up to 15 years after they have left the UK.

GOVERNMENT WORKING AT A LOCAL LEVEL

Central government, run by the Prime Minister and his Cabinet of Ministers, makes national policy decisions. However, at a local level, local authorities or councils manage local services for the local communities.

Local authorities or councils, which are run by elected members and public officials, make local policies and decisions and have a budget set by central government to spend on local needs. Having a second layer of government at local level demands rigorous arrangements and auditing to ensure public money is spent and managed properly by members who are fairly elected to the roles of councillors. A number of committees are formed within each council to monitor progress, decision-making and spending for such services as schools, environment, planning, etc.

Some decisions, such as the acceptance of policies and the budget, are reserved for the full council – this is where all the elected councillors meet to review and discuss plans. However, most decisions relating to the implementation of policy are for the executive (the paid public officials) within each council.

The executive is also responsible for preparing the policies and budget to propose to the authority or council. Decisions may be taken by:

- the executive collectively
- individual members of the executive
- committees of the executive
- officers of the authority.

Executives and councils are accountable to the local communities they serve. The executive is also able to delegate decision-making to area committees and to enter into partnership arrangements with other authorities.

The public, including the press, is admitted to meetings of the executive when key decisions are being discussed. They also have access to agendas, reports and minutes of meetings and certain background papers. In addition, local authorities must publish a forward plan setting out the decisions that will be taken over the coming months. Local authorities may exclude the public from meetings and withhold papers only in limited circumstances.

Local government powers

Local authorities work within the powers laid down under various Acts of Parliament at national government level. Their functions are far-reaching. Some are mandatory, which means that the authority must do what is required by law. Others are discretionary, allowing an authority to provide services if it wishes.

Local authorities operating within statutory restrictions

In certain cases, ministers have powers to secure uniformity in standards to safeguard public health or to protect the rights of individual citizens. Where local authorities exceed their statutory powers, they are regarded as acting outside the law and can be challenged in court.

The main link between local authorities and central government in England is the Office of the Deputy Prime Minister. However, other departments, such as the Department for Education and Skills, the Department for Work and Pensions, the Department of Health and the Home Office, are also concerned with various local government functions.

In Scotland, Wales and Northern Ireland, local authorities now deal mainly with the devolved Parliament and Assemblies.

About two million people are employed by local authorities in the UK. These include school teachers, the police, firefighters and other non-manual and manual workers. Education is the largest locally provided service, with 0.9 million full-time equivalent jobs. Councils are individually responsible, within certain legislative requirements, for deciding the structure of their workforces.

Every part of the UK is covered by a local authority fire service. Each of the 59 fire authorities must by law provide a firefighting service and must maintain a brigade to meet all normal requirements. Each fire authority appoints a Chief Fire Officer, or Firemaster in Scotland, who has day-to-day control of operations.

Local government elections

Local authorities consist of elected councillors, who are voted for in a way broadly similar to that for elections of Members of Parliament, except that proportional representation is used in Northern Ireland. Eligibility rules for voters are also similar to those for UK parliamentary elections, save that citizens of other member states of the EU may also vote.

To stand for election, candidates must either be registered as an elector or have some other close connection within the electoral area of their candidature, such as their principal place of employment. Councillors are paid a basic allowance, but may also be entitled to additional allowances and expenses for attending meetings or for taking on special responsibilities.

Whole council elections are held every four years in all county councils in England, borough councils in London, and about two-thirds of non-metropolitan district councils. In all other district councils, including the metropolitan districts, one-third of the councillors are elected in each of the three years when county council elections are not held. However, a few non-metropolitan district councils will soon hold biennial elections, with half of the councillors elected every two years. Whole council elections are every fourth year in Scotland, Wales and Northern Ireland.

The electoral arrangements of local authorities in England are kept under review by the Boundary Committee for England, established in April 2002 as a statutory committee of the Electoral Commission. Periodic electoral reviews of local authorities are undertaken in Scotland by the Local Government Boundary Commission for Scotland.

Mayors

Some districts have the ceremonial title of borough, or city, both granted by royal authority. Traditionally, councillors choose a Mayor (in Scotland a Provost) to act as presiding officer and to perform ceremonial duties. In the City of London and certain other large cities, he or she is known as the Lord Mayor. In Scotland, the presiding officer of the council of the four longest-established cities (Aberdeen, Dundee, Edinburgh and Glasgow) is called the Lord Provost.

The Local Government Act 2000 required local authorities in England and Wales to implement new decision-making structures, including the option of a directly elected mayor. Duties of mayors range from ceremonial to executive.

In most authorities the arrangements are based on one of three executive frameworks: a mayor and cabinet, a council leader and cabinet, or a mayor and council manager. Within these options, local authorities have considerable flexibility to work under a constitution that reflects local circumstances. Small shire district councils with a population of fewer than 85,000 have, in addition to executive arrangements, the choice of reforming their existing committee system. The majority of English and Welsh local authorities have opted for a style of executive where the leader of the cabinet is chosen by other councillors.

Provisions in the Local Government Act 2000 require councils in England and Wales to hold binding referendums if, following consultation, local people indicate that they want to elect a mayor directly under the new executive arrangements the Act put in place. Although the government has powers to direct a local authority to hold a referendum in certain circumstances, in June 2002 it announced that it would not intervene in cases where it did not agree with the judgement made by a council following consultation.

INTRODUCTION TO DEVOLUTION

The Labour government that came to power in 1997 committed to a decentralisation of power through the establishment of a Parliament and Executive in Scotland, an Assembly in Wales, and a longer-term devolution of power to regional level in England. The Belfast Agreement, reached in Northern Ireland in April 1998, approved in a referendum the following month, also paved the way for constitutional development.

Following the 'Machinery of Government changes' in June 2003, responsibility for the overall management of relations between the UK Government and the devolved administrations in Scotland, Wales and Northern Ireland has moved from the Office of the

Deputy Prime Minister (ODPM) to the Department for Constitutional Affairs (DCA). The ODPM remains responsible for the English region.

Prime Minister Tony Blair announced on 14 October 2002 that the full-time UK government posts of the Secretary of State for Scotland and Wales, following devolution, were no longer required and their roles could be combined with other posts. The Scottish and Welsh Offices were relocated within the new DCA, together with the Parliamentary Under-Secretaries of State for Scotland and Wales.

Scotland and Wales

The highest priority was given to the creation of a Parliament in Scotland and a National Assembly for Wales because the demand for decentralisation in these countries was stronger than in other parts of the UK.

The government published detailed proposals for Scotland and Wales in July 1997 and these were approved by referendums in Scotland and Wales in September of that year. The Scotland Act and the Government of Wales Act both completed their passage through the UK Parliament in 1998 and the first elections to the Scottish Parliament and the National Assembly for Wales took place on 6 May 1999. The devolution arrangements became fully operational on 1 July 1999.

Northern Ireland

The Secretary of State for Northern Ireland suspended the Northern Ireland Assembly on 14 October 2002 and Northern Ireland was returned to direct rule. The Secretary of State, assisted by his team of Northern Ireland Office Ministers, therefore assumed responsibility for the direction and control of the Northern Ireland Departments.

The Northern Ireland Assembly had been one of the new institutions created following the Belfast Agreement of April 1998. It was an Assembly of 108 members with a similar range of legislative and executive powers to the Scottish Parliament.

The Executive and the institutions were first set up on 2 December 1999, but were suspended when direct rule was re-introduced by the Secretary of State for Northern Ireland on 11 February 2000. The Executive and institutions were re-established following negotiations between all the parties on 29 May 2000. Devolution has been suspended on two further occasions, on 10 August and 21 September 2001, for 24 hours on each occasion.

England

In England, the government does not plan to impose a uniform system because demand for directly elected regional government varies considerably across the country.

In the first instance, the government has legislated to create Regional Development Agencies (RDAs) to promote economic development similar to Scottish Enterprise and the Welsh Development Agency. This legislation also provides for the establishment of regional chambers made up of members from local authorities in the region as well as including wide regional stakeholders from other sectors to co-ordinate transport, planning, economic development, bids for European funding and land use planning. The RDAs and the regional offices of central government are planned to work with the regional chambers.

The 1999 Greater London Authority Act created the Mayor of London and the London Assembly to restore strategic city-wide government for the capital.

The government published the White Paper on regional governance, *Your Region, Your Choice* on 9 May 2002. It proposed to strengthen the existing regional institutions in England, and take forward the government's manifesto commitment on elected regional government.

The Regional Assemblies (Preparations) Bill was introduced to Parliament on 14 November 2002. The Act received Royal Assent on 8 May 2003. The Act will take forward the commitment in the White Paper on regional governance to allow each of the English regions to establish an elected assembly, if approved in a referendum. This is the first of two pieces of primary legislation which will give effect to the Government's proposals for directly elected regional assemblies. This Act enables those regions that want to hold a referendum to have that chance.

The Greater London Authority

In May 2000, Londoners voted for a directly elected Mayor for the capital and for a separately elected Assembly of 25 members. Subsequent elections will take place every four years.

The Mayor and the London Assembly form the Greater London Authority (GLA), the first elected London-wide body since the Greater London Council (GLC) was abolished in 1986.

The Mayor of London sets key strategies on a range of London-wide issues, such as transport, economic development, strategic and spatial development and the environment. The Mayor also sets budgets for the GLA, Transport for London, the London Development Agency and the Metropolitan Police and London's fire services, and chairs Transport for London. The London Assembly scrutinises both the activities of the Mayor and issues of concern to Londoners.

In elections for London's mayor, voters are required to mark both their first and second choices on their ballot papers. If, in the first round, no candidate receives more than 50 per cent of the total votes cast, the second choices for the two leading candidates are added to their initial scores to decide the overall winner. For the Assembly elections, London is divided into 14 constituencies, whose members are elected using the 'first-past-the-post' system. A further 11 London-wide seats are allocated on a 'top-up' basis, whereby votes are counted across London and the seats are shared among the political parties in proportion to the votes each party receives.

Devolution in Scotland: overview

In a referendum held in September 1997, 74 per cent of those who voted endorsed the UK government's proposals to set up a Scottish Parliament and Executive to administer Scottish affairs. On a second question, on whether to give the new Parliament tax-varying powers, 64 per cent were in favour. The Scottish Parliament has a unique structure and wide responsibilities.

Legislation was introduced in the Westminster Parliament in December 1997 and the following November the Scotland Act 1998 passed into law. Elections to the first Scottish Parliament for almost 300 years were held in May 1999, and it met for the first time in July of that year.

Unlike the Westminster Parliament, the Scottish Parliament does not have a second chamber to revise legislation which comes before it. Detailed scrutiny of Bills is carried out in committees or by taking evidence from outside experts. The House of Lords no longer considers Scottish legislation on devolved matters, although it remains the final court of appeal in hearing civil cases arising from the Scottish courts.

The Scottish Parliament's 129 members (MSPs) are elected for a fixed four-year term. The Additional Member System of proportional representation is used in Scottish parliamentary elections, giving each voter two votes: one for a constituency MSP and one 'regional' vote for a registered political party or an individual independent candidate.

There are 73 single-member constituency seats and 56 seats representing eight regions (based on the European parliamentary constituencies), with each region returning seven members. These MSPs are allocated so that each party's overall share of seats in the Parliament reflects its share of the regional vote.

In June 2003, the Prime Minister, Tony Blair, announced that the role of Secretary of State for Scotland, to represent Scottish interests in the UK Cabinet, would be combined with other posts within the Cabinet.

The Scotland Office, together with the Wales Office, also moved to be part of the new Department for Constitutional Affairs. At Cabinet level, responsibility for the conduct of Scottish business, and lead responsibility for the representation of Scotland within the government and Parliament, will lie with a senior minister, supported by the staff located within the Department for Constitutional Affairs.

The Scottish Executive, the administrative arm of government in Scotland, has responsibility for all public bodies whose functions and services have been devolved to it, and is accountable to the Scottish Parliament for them.

The First Minister, normally the leader of the party with most support in the Parliament, heads the Scottish Executive. Since the first elections, the Executive has been run by a partnership between Labour and the Liberal Democrats, with the latter having two seats in the Cabinet of the Scottish Parliament, including that of Deputy First Minister. There are 11 Cabinet positions in all plus the non-elected Lord Advocate, the chief law officer.

Responsibilities of the Scottish Parliament

In certain areas, listed below, the Scottish Parliament is able to amend or repeal existing Acts of the UK Parliament and to pass new legislation of its own. The Scottish Parliament has the power to act in a wide number of areas.

Responsibility for a number of other issues, including overseas affairs, defence and national security, overall economic and monetary policy, energy, employment legislation and social security, anti-discrimination, asylum and immigration, remains with the UK government and Parliament as 'reserved' matters under Schedule 5 of the Scotland Act 1998.

The Scottish Parliament's areas of responsibility are:

- health
- education and training
- local government
- housing
- economic development
- many aspects of home affairs and civil and criminal law
- transport
- the environment
- agriculture, fisheries and forestry
- sport, culture and the arts.

The Northern Ireland Assembly and Executive: overview

The Secretary of State for Northern Ireland suspended the Northern Ireland Assembly on 14 October 2002 and Northern Ireland has been returned to direct rule.

Power and responsibility have been devolved to the Northern Ireland community. Prior to its suspension, the first elections for the Northern Ireland Assembly were held in June 1998, using the single transferable vote system of proportional representation. The 18 constituencies were the same as those for the UK Parliament, but each returned six MLAs (Members of the Legislative Assembly), giving the Assembly a total of 108 members.

At its first meeting in July 1998, the Assembly elected, on a cross-community basis, a First Minister and a Deputy First Minister, and appointed ten ministers with responsibility for each of the Northern Ireland departments, which together formed the Executive. These 12 ministers made up the Executive Committee, which met to discuss and agree on those issues that cut across the responsibilities of two or more ministers. Its role was to prioritise executive business and to recommend a common position, where necessary.

Following devolution, the Secretary of State for Northern Ireland – a member of the UK Cabinet whose main function was to ensure that the devolution settlement worked satisfactorily – remained responsible for Northern Ireland Office (NIO) matters not devolved to the Northern Ireland Assembly. These included policing, security policy, prisons and criminal justice.

The Assembly has been suspended on previous occasions. The Secretary of State for Northern Ireland re-introduced direct control of Northern Ireland on 11 February 2000. The Executive and institutions were re-established following negotiations between all the parties on 29 May 2000. Devolution has been suspended on two further occasions, on 10 August and 21 September 2001, for 24 hours on each occasion.

The arrangements for the Executive and the institutions will come back into force if and when the Assembly's current suspension is lifted.

Devolved powers and responsibilities

In December 1999, power to run most of Northern Ireland's domestic affairs was fully devolved by the Westminster Parliament to the Northern Ireland Assembly and its Executive Committee of Ministers. The Assembly met in Parliament Buildings at Stormont, Belfast, and was the prime source of authority for all devolved responsibilities. It had full legislative and executive powers within this framework, which meant it could make laws and take decisions on all the functions of the Northern Ireland departments.

The Executive's main function was to plan each year, and review as necessary, a programme of government with an agreed budget. This was subject to approval by the Assembly, after scrutiny in Assembly Committees, on a cross-community basis. MLAs could be on more than one Assembly Committee. The Assembly had ten Statutory Committees.

Membership of committees was in broad proportion to party strengths in the Assembly to ensure that the opportunity of committee places was available to all members. Each committee had a scrutiny, policy development and consultation role in relation to its department and a role in the initiation of legislation.

A 60-member Civic Forum, whose chairperson was appointed by the First Minister and Deputy First Minister, represented the business, trade union, voluntary and other sectors of the Northern Ireland community. It acted as a consultative mechanism on social, economic and cultural matters.

The Northern Ireland Office and the Assembly

The role of the Northern Ireland Office is to support the Secretary of State for Northern Ireland in securing a lasting peace, based on the Good Friday Agreement. When power has been devolved to the Northern Ireland Executive, the Secretary of State retains responsibility for constitutional and security issues as they relate to Northern Ireland, in particular law and order, political affairs, policing and criminal justice. Victims issues are handled by the NIO's Victims Liaison Unit and the NIO also has responsibility for matters relating to the licensing and legislation concerning firearms and explosives.

During devolution, economic and social matters are the responsibility of the Northern Ireland Executive. It handles policy relating to:

- agriculture and rural development
- culture, arts and leisure
- education, enterprise, trade and investment
- environment
- finance and personnel
- health
- social services and public safety
- higher and further education, training and employment
- regional development
- social development.

National Assembly for Wales and Welsh Assembly government: overview

In 1997, the Welsh people narrowly endorsed government proposals to devolve certain powers and responsibilities to a National Assembly. Of those who voted, 50.3 per cent were in favour.

The Welsh Assembly has wide-ranging powers and responsibilities

The Government of Wales Act 1998 laid down the necessary statutory framework to establish the National Assembly for Wales, which held its first elections in May 1999 and began functioning as a devolved administration two months later.

In February 2002, the National Assembly voted to make clear the difference in roles between ministers and the Assembly as a whole. The Welsh Assembly government develops and implements policy. It is accountable to the National Assembly and is primarily located in

Cathays Park, Cardiff. The National Assembly for Wales debates and approves legislation and holds the Assembly Government to account. Its debating chamber and members are located at Cardiff Bay.

Electors have two votes in Assembly elections: one for their local constituency and one for their electoral region. The Assembly comprises 60 members (AMs): 40 from local constituencies, with the same boundaries as those for Welsh seats in the House of Commons, and 20 regional members. The Assembly is elected by the Additional Member System of proportional representation.

The First Minister, who heads the Assembly government, is supported by a Cabinet of eight ministers in charge of economic development and transport, Assembly business, finance, local government and public services, education and lifelong learning, health and social care, social justice, housing and regeneration, environment, planning and countryside and culture, Welsh language and sport.

The Assembly is also responsible for more than 50 public bodies. These include the Welsh Development Agency, the Higher Education Funding Council for Wales, the Sports Council for Wales and the Welsh Language Board.

In June 2003, the Prime Minister announced that the role of Secretary of State for Wales, to represent Welsh interests in the UK Cabinet, would be combined with other posts within the Cabinet. The work of the Wales Office also moved to the new Department for Constitutional Affairs.

Powers of the National Assembly for Wales

The National Assembly for Wales only has powers to make secondary legislation, which it uses to meet distinctive Welsh needs. The Welsh Assembly exercises a range of specific responsibilities. Primary legislation on Welsh affairs continues to be made in the UK Parliament at Westminster.

Within Wales, the Assembly has power to develop and put into practice policies in the following areas:

- agriculture, forestry, fisheries and food
- ancient monuments and historic buildings
- culture
- economic development
- education and training
- the environment
- health and health services
- highways
- housing
- industry
- local government
- social services
- sport and recreation
- tourism
- town and country planning
- transport
- water and flood defence
- the Welsh language.

2

The UK as part of the European Union

WHAT IS THE EU?

The European Union (EU) is a family of democratic European countries, committed to working together for peace and prosperity. It is not a state intended to replace existing states, but it is more than any other international organisation. The EU is, in fact, unique. Its member states have set up common institutions to which they delegate some of their sovereignty so that decisions on specific matters of joint interest can be made democratically at European level. This pooling of sovereignty is also called 'European integration'.

The historical roots of the European Union lie in the Second World War. The idea of European integration was conceived to prevent such killing and destruction from ever happening again. It was first proposed by the French Foreign Minister Robert Schuman in a speech on 9 May 1950. This date, the 'birthday' of what is now the EU, is celebrated annually as Europe Day.

There are five EU institutions, each playing a specific role:

- European Parliament (elected by the peoples of the member states)
- Council of the European Union (representing the governments of the member states)

- European Commission (driving force and executive body)
- Court of Justice (ensuring compliance with the law)
- Court of Auditors (controlling sound and lawful management of the EU budget).

These are flanked by five other important bodies:

- European Economic and Social Committee (expresses the opinions of organised civil society on economic and social issues)
- Committee of the Regions (expresses the opinions of regional and local authorities)
- European Central Bank (responsible for monetary policy and managing the euro)
- European Ombudsman (deals with citizens' complaints about maladministration by any EU institution or body)
- European Investment Bank (helps achieve EU objectives by financing investment projects).

Several agencies and other bodies complete the system.

The rule of law is fundamental to the European Union. All EU decisions and procedures are based on treaties which are agreed by all the EU countries.

Initially, the EU consisted of just six countries: Belgium, Germany, France, Italy, Luxembourg and the Netherlands. Denmark, Ireland and the United Kingdom joined in 1973, Greece in 1981, Spain and Portugal in 1986, Austria, Finland and Sweden in 1995. In 2004 the biggest enlargement took place, with ten new countries joining.

In the early years, much of the co-operation between EU countries was about trade and the economy, but now the EU also deals with many other subjects of direct importance for everyday life, such as citizens' rights; ensuring freedom, security and justice; job creation; regional development; environmental protection; making globalisation work for everyone.

The European Union has delivered half a century of stability, peace and prosperity. It has helped to raise living standards, built a single Europe-wide market, launched the single European currency, the euro, and strengthened Europe's voice in the world.

Europe is a continent with many different traditions and languages, but also with shared values. The EU defends these values. It fosters co-operation among the peoples of Europe, promoting unity while preserving diversity and ensuring that decisions are taken as close as possible to the citizens.

In the increasingly interdependent world of the 21st century, it will be even more necessary for every European citizen to co-operate with people from other countries in a spirit of curiosity, tolerance and solidarity.

The purpose of the European Union

The European Union (EU) promotes social and economic progress among its members, common foreign and security positions, police and judicial co-operation in criminal matters, and European citizenship.

How the EU was formed

The EU's structure and operation are governed by a series of treaties. The 1957 Rome Treaty established the European Community, which the UK joined in 1973. Its aims were the creation of a common internal or single market, including an end to customs duties between member states, free movement of goods, people, services and capital, and an end to distortions in competition within this market. Most of the member states now use the single currency known as the euro (€).

These aims were reaffirmed by the 1986 Single European Act, which introduced measures to complete the single market. Under the Rome Treaty, the European Commission speaks on behalf of the UK and the other member states in international trade negotiations.

The 1992 Maastricht Treaty amended the Rome Treaty and made other commitments, including moves towards economic and monetary union. It established the European Union, which comprises the European Community and intergovernmental arrangements for a Common Foreign and Security Policy (CFSP) as well as for increased co-operation on justice and home affairs policy issues.

The Maastricht Treaty also introduced the principle of subsidiarity, which means that, in areas where the Community and member states share competence, action should be taken at European level only if its objectives cannot be achieved by member states acting alone and can be better achieved by the Community. The Treaty also introduced the concept of EU citizenship to supplement national citizenship.

The Amsterdam Treaty, in force from 1999, introduced:

- the further protection and extension of citizens' rights
- integration of the 'social chapter', previously a separate protocol to the Maastricht Treaty, into the treaty framework following its adoption by the UK
- new mechanisms to improve the operation of the CFSP
- an increase in the areas subject to co-decision between the Council of Ministers and European Parliament
- simplification of the co-decision procedure.

The Nice Treaty, which was signed in February 2001, introduced changes to the EU's institutional machinery in preparation for enlargement. From 2005, the number of votes for each EU country in the Council of the European Union was altered to take account of prospective new members, the total number rising from the 87 votes for the current 25 member states up to 345 votes for 27 member states.

The UK, Germany, France and Italy will each have 29 votes. The total needed for a qualified majority will increase from 62 to 255, and for a blocking minority from 26 to 91, in an EU of 27 member states. Qualified majority voting will be extended to 35 more areas, including trade in some services, aspects of asylum and immigration policy, and regulation of the European Court of Justice. From 2005, the European Commission was composed of one member from each country, up to 27.

Any amendments to treaties must be agreed unanimously and must then be ratified by each member state according to its own constitutional procedures. In the UK, treaty ratifications must be approved by Parliament before they can come into force.

EU SIZE AND KEY FIGURES AT A GLANCE

The European Union (EU) covers a large part of the continent of Europe, from the Arctic Circle to the Mediterranean and from the Atlantic to the Aegean.

Though richly diverse, the countries that make up the EU (its 'member states') are all committed to the same fundamental values: peace, democracy, the rule of law and respect for human rights. They seek to promote these values, to build and share prosperity and to exert their collective influence by acting together on the world stage.

Over half a century, the Union has raised its citizens' standard of living to unprecedented levels. It has created a frontier-free single market and a single currency, the euro. It is a major economic power and the world leader in development aid. Its membership has grown from six to 25 nations.

EU Member States

Austria
Belgium
Cyprus
Czech Republic
Denmark
Estonia
Finland
France
Germany
Greece
Hungary
Ireland
Italy
Latvia
Lithuania
Luxembourg
Malta
Poland
Portugal
Slovakia
Slovenia
Spain
Sweden
The Netherlands
United Kingdom

In 2006, the following 'candidate countries' were waiting to join as member states:

Bulgaria	Turkey
Romania	Croatia

Before a candidate country can join the EU it must have a stable system of democratic government and institutions that ensure the rule of law and respect for human rights. It must also have a functioning and competitive market economy.

The EU today faces new challenges, not least globalisation. To become more competitive while remaining a fair and caring community, the EU needs to get more people into new and better jobs and to give them new skills.

Detailed statistics about the European Union are published by Eurostat, the EU's statistical office. See their website, where more than 1,000 tables of statistics can be accessed free of charge. http://epp.eurostat.cec.eu.int

A major trading power

Seen on a map of the world, the EU is not a huge area. However, it has the world's third largest population, after China and India. The United States covers an area nearly three times bigger than the EU, but it has fewer people.

The developed world's share of the total human population is steadily shrinking, while the less developed countries' share is growing. This is a matter for real concern, and one reason why the EU intends to continue its efforts to promote global development. It is already the world's leading supplier of development aid.

Facts and figures

- The European Union has about 457 million inhabitants – the world's third largest population after China and India and accounts for some 7 per cent of the total world population.
- It accounts for almost a fifth of global imports and exports
- In all EU countries over 60 per cent of Gross Domestic Product (GDP) is generated by the service sector, i.e. banking, tourism, transport and insurance.

For detailed information about the EU go to http://europa.eu.int/, where the site is translated into 20 languages.

THE UK AS A MEMBER STATE

As a member state of the European Union, the UK is bound by the various types of European Community (EC) legislation and wider policies that are based on a series of treaties since the 1950s. Almost all UK government departments are involved in EU-wide activities.

The Council of the European Union is the main decision-making body

The Community enacts legislation that is binding on the national governments of the 25 member states or, in certain circumstances, on individuals and companies within those states. UK government ministers take part in the discussions and decision-making. The final decision is taken collectively by all the member states.

The UK Representative Office (UKREP), based in Brussels, conducts most of the negotiations on behalf of the UK government. Following UK devolution, offices were opened in Brussels to promote the interests of Scotland and Wales within the EU. Both work in close co-operation with UKREP.

The Council of the European Union is the main decision-making body. Member states are represented by the ministers appropriate to the subject under discussion. When, for instance, education matters are being discussed, the UK's Secretary of State for Education and Skills attends with his or her European counterparts. The Presidency of the Council changes at six-monthly intervals and rotates in turn among the 25 member states of the Union.

In some cases, Council decisions must be unanimous. In others, they are taken by qualified majority voting (a qualified majority being the number of votes required for a decision to be adopted), with votes weighted according to a country's population – currently ten each for Germany, France, the United Kingdom and Italy, eight for Spain, five each for Belgium, Greece, the Netherlands and Portugal, four each for Austria and Sweden, three each for Denmark, Finland and the Irish Republic, and two for Luxembourg. The threshold for the qualified majority is set at 62 votes out of 87.

The European Council usually meets twice a year and comprises the heads of state or government (accompanied by their foreign ministers), the President of the European Commission and one other commissioner. The Council defines general political guidelines.

The European Commission is the executive body. It implements the Council's decisions, initiates legislation and ensures that member states put it into effect. Each of the 20 commissioners, who are drawn from all member states (there are two from the UK), is responsible for a specific policy area, for example, education, transport or agriculture.

The commissioners are entirely independent of their countries and serve the EU as a whole.

THE EUROPEAN PARLIAMENT

The European Parliament, which has 732 directly elected members (MEPs), including 78 from the UK, plays an increasingly important role in the legislative process.

The Parliament is consulted about major decisions and has substantial shared power with the Council of the European Union over the EC budget. In areas of legislation its role varies between:

- consultation, where it can influence but does not have the final say in the content of legislation
- co-operation and assent procedures, where its influence is greater
- co-decision, introduced by the Maastricht Treaty and extended in the Amsterdam Treaty, where a proposal requires the agreement of both the Council and the European Parliament.

The Parliament meets in full session in Strasbourg for about one week every month, although its committee work normally takes place in Brussels.

Elections to the European Parliament take place every five years, the most recent being in June 2004. In the UK, these were held under a proportional representation system, bringing the country into line with the other member states.

Some EC legislation is issued jointly by the Council of the European Union and the European Parliament, some by the Council and some by the Commission under delegated powers. It consists of Regulations, Directives and Decisions:

- Regulations are directly applicable in all member states and have the force of law without the need for implementing further measures.
- Directives are equally binding as to the result to be achieved, but allow each member state to choose the form and method of implementation.
- Decisions, like Regulations, do not normally need national implementing legislation. They are binding on those to whom they are addressed.

Each member state provides one of the judges to serve in the European Court of Justice, which is the final authority on all aspects of Community law. Its rulings must be applied by member states, and fines can be imposed on those failing to do so. The Court is assisted by a Court of First Instance, which handles certain cases brought by individuals and companies. The UK is also represented on the Court of Auditors, which examines Community revenue and expenditure, to see that it is legally received and spent.

For more information about the EU Parliament visit http://www.europarl.eu.int/, where the site is translated into 20 languages and covers all the detailed information you need to know about the EU parliament.

PART TWO

3

Managed migration

Immigration and more specifically economic migration have become a phenomenon of globalisation. Some workers now work in the 'global village'. These are contract workers and other professionals. Some multi-national employers expect that new hires can demonstrate some time living a different country and culture before they will make an offer of employment.

A skilled person can now use the Internet to market their skills anywhere in the world. Likewise, employers can search and identify the candidates they need. This will change candidate search and selection, and how commerce and industry will operate this century.

However, with the ongoing threat of terrorism, governments worldwide will continue to manage immigration policies to ensure they keep a tight grip on their national security.

In the run-up to the 2005 election, the UK government released its paper *Making Migration Work for Britain*. The coined term 'managed migration' reflected the government approach. The paper outlined their five-year strategy. This gives an idea on their thinking and the future of immigration policy for the UK.

Foreign immigration to Britain was just under 500,000 in 2004. As UK employers find it more difficult to fill job vacancies, it is not surprising that employers are looking abroad to find candidates.

Current figures show that more than eight in ten UK employers now recruit staff from overseas. However, bringing staff into the UK can be complicated.

This book focuses mainly on what we call the economic and family migration routes into the UK. Humanitarian categories are different specialisms. The content of this book will not cover information for applicants under political asylum and refugee categories. People needing any assistance in this area should make contact with the JCWI (Joint Council for the Welfare of Immigrants), www.jcwi.org.uk.

The five-year strategy is the next stage of the government's comprehensive reform of the immigration and asylum policies and procedures. The purpose of the reforms is to admit people selectively in order to ensure maximum economic benefits from migration to the UK. Migration makes a substantial contribution to economic growth; helps fill gaps in the labour market, which includes key public services such as education and health, and increases investment, innovation and fosters new business in the UK.

The government is sending out a message that it wants to make it easier for employers to access the skills and experience they need and for the education sector to attract international students.

Currently there are broadly three classes of migrants in the managed migration system:

1. short term, temporary categories – visitors, business visitors, students

2. employment categories – work permit holders, and a range of permit free categories including, for example, overseas journalists
3. family categories – for marriage, or to join parents or children.

Highly skilled, high-earning migrants are important to the continuing development of the UK as a high-value economy. Skilled migrants contribute through their own productivity and related 'spillover' effects, that is, by transferring their knowledge and skills to UK workers. Similarly, the ability to hire workers from abroad is important in making the UK an attractive business environment for firms setting up and remaining in the UK.

In 2001–02, international students in UK further and higher institutions, English-language training providers and independent schools contributed an estimated £5 billion, in tuition fees and other spending, making it a significant contributor to the UK economy (*The Global Value of Education and Training Exports to the UK Economy*, British Council, 2004).

The government has moved to regulate and license the education sector and made numerous changes to the rules on how to get a visa to study in the UK. If you have been a genuine student applicant to one of the British Missions abroad, you may not have found them very welcoming when you applied for the necessary visa, reflecting current legislation.

The current system has developed over time. Immigration rules, made under section 3(2) of the Immigration Act 1971, are the statement laid before Parliament to regulate the entry and stay of people, subject to immigration control, in the UK. These rules cover visits, study, work, family reunion, asylum, appeal rights, and removal and deportation. The rules were last consolidated in May 1994 (HC 395) and have undergone 41 changes since then. There are some 50 different ways to come to the UK to work or study. Of these, the main Work Permit system and the Highly Skilled Migrant Programme (HSMP) have been used most for delivering the desired outcomes for the UK.

As you read through the following pages you should expect to find initial information on whether you meet basic criteria for the more popular categories used for people to visit, live, work and study in the UK.

The government review on managed migration identified the case for designing a new system for the UK for the 21st century, which was announced in the five-year strategy in February 2005. Their proposals outlined that there should be five tiers in the managed migration system, to reflect the purposes of different migrants in coming to the UK. The purposes were defined as follows:

1. Tier 1: Highly Skilled individuals to contribute to growth and productivity.
2. Tier 2: Skilled workers with a job offer; and workers to meet specific overseas requirements.
3. Tier 3: Limited numbers of workers to fill low-skill shortages.
4. Tier 4: Students: increasing exports and improving the education sector for the UK.
5. Tier 5: Other temporary categories: visiting workers, selected development schemes and youth mobility/cultural exchange.

It is probably worth mentioning at this stage that most governments have the best of intentions when developing new policy. They even go to great lengths to consult with stakeholders. However, as we see too many times, the new policy may not have been fully thought out and once it has been introduced may well fail to deliver the required outcomes.

Each applicant will have different personal circumstances so no two cases are ever exactly the same. Much can be left to the determination of an Entry Clearance Officer, who has the final say in deciding your case after consideration – no visa and you will have no entry. Even worse is the government's move towards removing any right of appeal in certain categories.

CITIZENSHIP

The government intends to make gaining British citizenship meaningful and celebratory rather than being a bureaucratic process. New citizenship ceremonies are now part of the process. The government is also keen that those who become British citizens should play an active role, both economic and political, in our society, and have a sense of belonging to a wider community. All adults who want to become a British citizen need to demonstrate their knowledge of life in the UK by successfully completing the new 'Life in the UK' test from November 2005.

Most of the information needed for the test can be found in this book.

4

The Highly Skilled Migrant Programme

WHAT IS THE HIGHLY SKILLED MIGRANT PROGRAMME?

The Highly Skilled Migrant Programme (HSMP) has been designed to allow highly skilled people to migrate to the United Kingdom to look for work or self-employment opportunities. The scheme has two categories, one for applicants aged under 28 and another for those aged 28 and over.

The Highly Skilled Migrant Programme does not require you to have a specific job offer in the UK to apply. It is different from business routes because you do not need a detailed business plan; you do not need to create jobs; and you do not need to invest in the UK.

How do I apply for Highly Skilled Migrant Visa?

You are required to apply directly to the Highly Skilled Migrant Programme Team at Work Permits (UK). You are able to apply from abroad. In most cases, you can also apply from inside the UK if you are here with Home Office permission.

Your application will not be successful if you are in the United Kingdom as a visitor, on temporary admission, or without permission.

How do I qualify as a Highly Skilled Migrant?

The Highly Skilled Migrant Programme is a points-based immigration scheme. Points are scored in five main areas:

- educational qualifications
- work experience
- past earnings
- your achievement in your chosen field
- your husband's, wife's or unmarried partner's achievements.

A total of 65 points is required in order to qualify for this scheme.

Under-28 category

If you are under 28 years of age, you are able to score points by providing evidence of the following.

Educational background

In this category you can score the following points depending to the educational qualifications you hold:

PhD	Master's (e.g. MBA)	Graduate degree (e.g. BA or BSc)
30	25	15

Work experience

In this category you are able to score points by providing evidence of the following:

At least two years full-time graduate-level work experience	At least four years full-time graduate-level work experience	At least four years full-time graduate-level work experience including at least 1 year in a senior or specialist role
25	35	50

Points will only be awarded for this section where sufficient original evidence has been provided to satisfy the HSMP team that the post has clearly demonstrated either graduate, senior or specialist level experience. The evidence should also demonstrate that the applicant has worked in the post(s) on a full-time basis for the required length of time.

Past earnings

The past earnings requirements for under-28s assessment are broadly equivalent to the top 10 per cent earnings of all full-time workers in this age group. In order to score points in this category you need to demonstrate a minimum earned income in your country of residence over the 12 months prior to the application being made. In order to reflect differences in income levels across the world, the level required to qualify varies depending on where you have been living. The country where you have been residing and working over this period, rather than your nationality, determines the income band.

You can find up-to-date information regarding your ability to claim points in this section by visiting www.workingintheuk.gov.uk.

Over-28 category

If you are aged 28 years or more, you are able to score points by providing evidence of the following.

Educational background

In this category you can score the following according to the educational qualifications you hold:

PhD	Master's (e.g. MBA)	Graduate degree (e.g. BA or BSc)
30	25	15

Work experience

In this category you are able to score points by providing evidence of the following:

At least five years full-time graduate-level work experience (or three years if you have a PhD)	At least five years full-time graduate-level work experience including at least two years in a senior or specialist role	At least ten years full-time graduate-level work experience including at least five years in a senior or specialist role
25	35	50

Past earnings

The past earnings requirements for the 28s and over assessment are broadly equivalent to the top 10 per cent earnings of all full-time workers in this age group. In order to score points in this category you need to demonstrate a minimum earned income in your country of residence over the 12 months prior to the application being made. In order to reflect differences in income levels across the world, the level required to qualify varies depending on where you live. The country you have been residing and working in over this period, rather than your nationality, determines the income band.

You can find up-to-date information regarding your ability to claim points in this section by visiting www.workingintheuk.gov.uk.

Points awarded within both categories

Within both categories you are able to claim the following points.

Achievement in your chosen field

Points awarded for this section:

Significant achievement	Exceptional achievement
15	25

Examples of this could be:

- a breakthrough in your field of expertise, e.g. a piece of original published research that is recognised as this in your field of expertise
- a recognised artistic achievement
- a lifetime achievement award from an industry body
- an invention which has been commercially successful.

Partners' achievements

Points awarded for this section:

Spouse/unmarried partner educated to degree level or previously employed in a graduate-level job and lived together for two years or more
10

In order to score in this category, you must provide evidence that your spouse or unmarried partner is educated to degree level (e.g. BA or BSc) or an equivalent vocational or professional qualification.

Alternatively, you can provide evidence that they are currently or have previously been employed in a graduate-level job. Your spouse or partner must accompany or join you in the UK. In addition, your spouse or partner must not already have been granted settlement (permanent residence) in the UK.

It is essential that at least three pieces of evidence are supplied in support of your partnership, and that these should cover a period of no less than two years.

MBA criteria

To meet the requirements of the MBA provision, to qualify for HSMP approval, you must:

- Have graduated from an eligible MBA programme. The first list was published on 2 December 2004, so the earliest eligible graduation date will be 2 December 2004. The date of graduation will be taken as the date on the graduation certificate.
- Provide evidence that clearly demonstrates you have graduated from an eligible MBA programme. The MBA course must have been completed. You cannot apply for this provision while part-way through the MBA programme.

If you provide sufficient evidence of your MBA qualification and this was awarded at an eligible institution and the HSMP team is satisfied that you meet the requirements of the scheme, you will automatically be awarded 65 points, the HSMP passmark.

You can find up-to-date information regarding your ability to claim points in this section by visiting www.workingintheuk.gov.uk.

HOW LONG WILL I BE ALLOWED TO STAY IN THE UK AS A HIGHLY SKILLED MIGRANT?

Initially, you are given permission to stay in the UK for 24 months to seek work or self-employment opportunities. At the end of this period you are able to apply to extend your stay as long as you are able to show evidence that you have been economically active.

As a Highly Skilled Migrant, can I stay in the UK permanently?

If you live in the UK continuously for five years with Home Office permission, you can apply toward the end of this five years for permission to remain in the UK indefinitely.

CAN MY FAMILY JOIN ME IN THE UK?

Your husband, wife, or eligible partner and children under 18 years of age can join you in the UK if:

- they have a visa for this purpose
- you can support them and live without any help from public funds.

5

Work permit approved employment

If you are a non-EEA (European Economic Area) national and are offered a position of employment in the UK, the company that wishes to employ you is first required to apply for permission to do so – if they are successful you will be issued with a work permit.

COMPANY REQUIREMENTS

The following criteria need to be met by the company that wishes to make this application.

- A company can make a work permit applications if they are a UK-based employer and need to employ a person to work in the UK.
- If a company wishes to employ a person, it will need to do so on a Class 1 National Insurance basis.
- While in the UK the Home Office expects the person to be the company's employee. There should be a contract of employment between employer and employee. The contract of employment can be requested at the time of your application.
- If the person is being transferred from an overseas parent or subsidiary branch of the company or is being seconded from an overseas company, it may be appropriate for the overseas contract of employment to continue; however, it must be clear that there is an employer/employee relationship between the UK-based company and the person.

- There must be a genuine vacancy. The post must not have been created for the purpose of recruiting a particular person. The Home Office must be satisfied that enough work exists for the person to undertake for the amount of hours and period that the company has requested.

- A work permit is issued where it is clear that the company applying has a clear responsibility for determining the duties and functions of the post. A company may apply for a work permit for a person who will be employed to provide services to a client under a contract, which may mean that the person will need to work at the client's premises. Work Permits (UK) will not issue a work permit where the employer is only supplying personnel. If this is the case, the company will need to demonstrate that they are responsible for the delivery of a particular job, project or piece of work with which the vacancy is associated. If the application involves providing a service to a client under a contract, a copy of this contract will be required at the time of application.

- The pay and conditions offered to the overseas national must be equal to those normally given to a resident worker doing similar work.

- The employment complies with UK legislation and any requirements for registration or licensing necessary for the employment and the company has ensured that they and their employee have obtained any necessary registration or licensing.

INDIVIDUAL REQUIREMENTS

For an individual to qualify for a work permit, the job they have been offered must meet the following criteria:

EITHER – the job must require the following qualifications:

- a UK equivalent degree level qualification; or
- a Higher National Diploma (HND)-level qualification which is relevant to the post on offer; or
- an HND level qualification, which is not relevant to the post on offer plus one year of relevant full-time work experience at National/Scottish Vocational Qualification (N/SVQ) level 3 or above.

OR the job must require the following skills:

- Three years' full-time experience of using specialist skills acquired through doing the type of job for which the permit is sought. This should be at N/SVQ level 3 or above.

There are several different categories in which work permit applications can be made – it is advisable to contact a registered immigration agent to ascertain which of these the company/ candidate fit into before proceeding.

6

Spouses, fiancé/es and unmarried partners

HOW DO I QUALIFY TO JOIN MY SPOUSE OR PARTNER IN THE UK?

You qualify if you can prove that:

- you are legally married to each other or are in a *de facto* partnership recognised in the UK
- your spouse or partner is present and settled in the UK*
- you intend to live together permanently as spouses or *de facto* partners
- you have met each other before
- together you can support yourselves and any dependants without assistance from public funds
- you have suitable accommodation, which is owned or lived in only by you and your household, and where you and your dependants can live without any assistance from public funds
- your spouse or partner is not under 18
- you are not under 18.

If you have more than one wife or husband, only one will be allowed to join you in the UK.

---

* 'Settled' means being allowed to live in the UK lawfully, with no time limit on your stay. 'Present and settled' means that the person concerned is settled in the UK and, at the time your application is made is either in the UK or is intending to coming here with you, or to join you and plans to live with you in the UK if your application is successful.

Initially, you will be allowed to stay and work in the UK for two years. Towards the end of this period, if you are still married and intend to continue living together, you are able to make an application to the Immigration and Nationality Directorate to stay in the UK permanently.

If you and your spouse or *de facto* partner have been living together outside the UK for four years or more, and they have been a British citizen for four years or more, there is no limit on the time you can stay in the UK.

HOW DO I QUALIFY TO JOIN MY FIANCÉ, FIANCÉE OR PROPOSED PARTNER IN THE UK?

You qualify if you can prove that:

- you plan to marry or register a civil partnership within a reasonable time (usually six months)
- you intend to live together permanently after you are married or have registered a civil partnership
- you have met each other before
- there is somewhere for you and your dependants to live until you get married or register a civil partnership, and you will be able to live without assistance from public funds
- you and your dependants can be supported without working or claiming any assistance from public funds.

You will be allowed to stay in the UK for six months but do not have permission to take employment within this period. When you are married or have registered a civil partnership, you can apply for a two-year extension to your visa and, if your application is granted, you will be allowed to take employment witout restriction. Towards the end of this period, you are able to make an application to the Immigration and Nationality Directorate to stay in the UK permanently.

HOW DO I QUALIFY TO JOIN MY UNMARRIED OR SAME-SEX PARTNER IN THE UK?

You qualify if you can prove that:

- your partner currently lives and is settled in the UK, or that they are going to live permanently in the UK
- both you and your partner are over 18 years of age

and

- any previous marriages or civil partnerships have permanently broken down
- you have been living together in a relationship similar to marriage or civil partnership for two years or more
- you have suitable accommodation which is owned or lived in only by you and your household, and where you and your dependants can live without any assistance from public funds
- you can support yourselves and any dependants without any help from public funds
- you intend to live together permanently
- both you and your partner are over 18 years of age.

Initially, you will be allowed to stay and work in the UK for two years. Towards the end of this period, if you are still married and intend to continue living together, you are able to make an application to the Immigration and Nationality Directorate to stay in the UK permanently.

If you and your unmarried or same-sex partner have been living together outside the UK for four years or more, and they have been a British citizen for four years or more, there will be no time limit on how long you can stay in the UK.

7

EEA nationals

The following countries are members of the European Economic Area (EEA):

Austria	Hungary	Netherlands
Belgium	Iceland	Norway
Cyprus	Ireland	Poland
Czech Republic	Italy	Portugal
Denmark	Latvia	Slovakia
Estonia	Liechtenstein	Slovenia
Finland	Lithuania	Spain
France	Luxembourg	Sweden
Germany	Malta	United Kingdom
Greece		

DO I HAVE A RIGHT OF RESIDENCE IN THE UK?

European Community law gives EEA nationals a right to live and work in the UK. This is called a right of residence.

You have the right of residence in the UK if you are an EEA national and:

- you are working in the UK, or
- you do not work in the UK but you have enough money to support yourself for the whole period of your stay without assistance from public funds.

How do I prove my nationality when entering the UK?

You will need to show your passport or national identity card. When you arrive at UK ports and airports you should use the separate channel marked 'EEA/EU' where it is available. Immigration officers will check your passport or national identity card to make sure that it is valid and that it belongs to you.

WHAT RIGHTS DO I HAVE IF I WANT TO WORK IN THE UK?

You can:

- accept offers for work
- work (in employment or self-employment)
- set up in business
- manage a company
- set up a local branch of a company.

You do not need a work permit, but you may need to register as a worker under the Worker Registration Scheme.

Can I live in the UK if I am not working?

You can live in the UK without working, for example as a student or a retired person. You must have enough money to support yourself through the whole period of your stay so that you do not need assistance from public funds.

Can I work in the UK if I am studying?

Yes. You can work in the UK during or after finishing your studies although you may need to register as a worker under the Worker Registration Scheme.

Do I need to apply for a residence permit or register with the police?

No. If you have the right to live in the UK, you can stay for as long as you want without getting a residence permit, or registering with the police. However, if you choose to do so, you can apply to the Immigration and Nationality Directorate for a residence permit. This simply confirms that you have the right to live in the UK under European Community law.

A residence permit is normally valid for five years. However, one may be issued for shorter periods if you are working or studying in the UK for less than 12 months.

You will not normally be granted a residence permit if you:

- are in the UK for a short visit
- are looking for work
- will work and live in the UK for less than three months
- do not work in the UK and you cannot support yourself without help from public funds
- have been registered on the Worker Registration Scheme for less than 12 months.

YOUR FAMILY'S RIGHTS

If your family members are EEA nationals they will have the same rights as you to live and work in the UK.

The following information applies to family members who are not EEA nationals.

Can my family join me in the UK?

Yes. If you have the right to live in the UK, your family can join you. Under European Community law, your family includes:

- your spouse
- your spouse's children or grandchildren (if they are under 21 years of age or if they are over 21 and are dependent on you)
- dependent relatives, for example your spouse's parents or grandparents.

If you are a student, only your husband or wife and your dependent children can join you.

An unmarried partner is not eligible for an EEA family permit.

Can my other relatives join me in the UK?

Your other relatives, such as brothers, sisters, cousins and so on, do not have an automatic right to live in the UK with you. However, applications will be considered if you are working or coming to work in the UK and:

- they are dependent on you
- they were living with you before you came to the UK
- they are living with you now outside of the UK.

How can my family come to live with me in the UK?

Non-EEA family members must obtain an EEA family permit before they travel to the UK if they are coming to live with you permanently or on a long-term basis. If they try to enter the UK for this purpose without an EEA family permit, they may be refused entry. An EEA family permit is a form of entry clearance that allows members of your family who are not EEA nationals to travel with you or join you in the UK.

Can my family members take employment in the UK?

Yes. A family member of an EEA national who is exercising their rights under EU law can take employment.

Can my family lose their right to stay in the UK?

Your family could lose their right of residence in the UK if:

- you no longer have the right of residence in the UK
- you leave the UK permanently
- you are not working in the UK and you cannot live in the UK without getting help from public funds.

Your husband or wife may also lose the right to stay in the UK if you are divorced.

Do I have to be present when my family members apply for a family permit?

No. As long as your family member has all of the relevant documents, they can apply without you needing to be present.

8

The Working Holidaymaker Scheme

WHAT IS THE WORKING HOLIDAYMAKER SCHEME?

The Working Holidaymaker Scheme is an arrangement, where Commonwealth citizens between the ages of 17 and 30 can come to the UK for an extended holiday of up to two years. You are able to take employment but this should be incidental. The holiday should be the main reason for your stay.

HOW DO I QUALIFY?

To qualify and obtain a Working Holidaymaker visa you must be able to show that you:

- are a Commonwealth citizen, a British Overseas Territories citizen, a British Overseas citizen or a British National (Overseas)
- are aged between 17 and 30
- want to come to the UK for an extended holiday, and intend to take employment as part of your holiday for no more than 12 months during your stay
- do not intend to set yourself up in or run a business, or work as a professional sportsperson during your stay
- are single, or are married to someone who also qualifies as a working holidaymaker and you plan to take the working holiday together
- do not have any dependent children aged five or over, or who will be five before your holiday ends

- can support yourself and live in the UK without needing any help from public funds
- have not spent time in the UK on a previous working holidaymaker visa
- intend to leave the UK at the end of your holiday.

You must make your application to the British High Commission and this must have been approved and your visa endorsed in your passport before you attempt to travel to the United Kingdom.

HOW LONG CAN I STAY?

You are allowed to stay in the UK for up to two years from the date you were first given permission to enter as a working holidaymaker. Any time you spend outside the UK during that period will be counted as part of the two years.

HOW MUCH AND WHAT TYPE OF EMPLOYMENT CAN I UNDERTAKE?

Employment in the UK must not be the main reason for your holiday, so you must spend no more than 12 months in employment, paid or unpaid.

You can undertake most types of work, including voluntary work, but you are not allowed to set yourself up in or run a business, or work as a professional sportsperson. You may choose when to work and when to take your holiday breaks, but you must not work for more than a total of 12 months of the two-year period or you will be breaking the conditions of your stay.

9

Visas and residency

WHAT IS A VISA?

A visa is a certificate that is put into your passport or travel document at a British Mission overseas. The visa gives you permission to enter the UK. If you have a valid UK visa you will not normally be refused entry to the UK unless your circumstances have changed, or you have provided false information or you did not disclose important facts when you applied for your visa.

When you arrive in the UK, an immigration officer may ask you questions; therefore it is advisable to have all relevant documentation in your hand luggage.

STUDENT VISA

How do I qualify to travel to the UK as a student?

To qualify to travel to the UK as a student you must be able to prove that you have been accepted on a course of study at an educational establishment that is on the UK's Department for Education and Skills (DfES) Register of Education and Training Providers. You are able to search this register on the DfES website at www.dfes.gov.uk/providersregister.

You must be able to show that you are going to register on one of the following:

- a recognised full-time degree course

- a course run during the week involving at least 15 hours of organised daytime study each week
- a full-time course at an independent fee-paying school.

In addition you must:

- be able to pay for your course and support yourself and any dependants, and live in the UK without working full time (part-time employment is allowed) or any help from public funds
- intend to leave the UK when you complete your studies.

You must make your application to the relevant British Mission and this must have been approved and a visa endorsed in your passport before you attempt to travel to the United Kingdom.

If you are a student who successfully completes a degree course while in the UK, you may be able to switch into work permit-approved employment, if you meet the requirements.

Can I extend my stay as a student?

If you enter the UK with a student or prospective student visa, or you want to study on a course at degree level or higher, you can apply for an extension of stay to the Immigration and Nationality Directorate, which is a part of the Home Office. The Immigration and Nationality Directorate will charge you a fee for any extension to your stay.

The maximum period of time that a student can stay in the UK on short courses one after the other, below degree level, is two years. If you did not enter the UK with a student or prospective student visa or are not studying on a degree-level course or higher, you will not be allowed to extend your stay.

Can I take employment?

You can take part-time or holiday work, but you must not:

- work for more than 20 hours per week during term time unless your placement is part of your studies and has been agreed with your education institution and leads to a degree or qualification awarded by a nationally recognised examining body
- do business, be self-employed or provide services as a professional sportsperson or entertainer
- work full-time in a permanent job.

If you are coming to the UK as a student for six months or less, you must ask the entry clearance officer for permission to work.

Can I switch to work permit employment when I am in the UK?

You may be able to switch if:

- you have completed a recognised degree course at either a UK publicly funded institution of further or higher education, or an approved private education institution that has satisfactory records of enrolment and attendance
- you hold a valid work permit for employment
- you have the written consent of any government or agency that is sponsoring you
- you have not broken immigration law.

Can I bring my spouse and children with me?

Your spouse and any of your children under 18 can come to the UK with you during your studies, as long as you can support them and live without needing help from public funds.

Will my spouse be allowed to take employment?

Your husband or wife will be allowed to work in the UK if you receive permission to stay in the UK for 12 months or more.

Am I allowed to travel to the UK to arrange my studies?

You can travel to the UK as a prospective student for up to six months to arrange your studies. You will need to show that:

- you intend to enrol on a course of study within six months of arriving in the UK
- you can pay for your course, support yourself and your dependants, and live without working or needing any help from public funds
- you intend to leave the UK when you finish your studies or when your permission to stay ends if you do not qualify to stay in the UK as a student.

ANCESTRY VISA

How do I qualify for UK ancestry?

You qualify if you can prove that:

- you are a Commonwealth citizen
- you are aged 17 or over
- you have a grandparent who was born in the UK, the Channel Islands or the Isle of Man

- you have a grandparent who was born in what is now the Republic of Ireland before 31 March 1922
- you are able to work and intend to do so in the UK
- you can support yourself and any dependants, and live without needing any help from public funds.

NB: If you or your parent (through whom you are claiming ancestry) are adopted, you are still able to apply for entry under this category. You must show evidence of the legal adoption with your application form.

Do I need to obtain a work permit?

No. You do not need a work permit.

How long can I stay?

If you arrive with a UK ancestry visa, you have permission to stay for an initial period of two years. After two years, you will be able to apply for an extension for a further three years to allow you to complete the required five-year period before applying for permanent residence.

You can apply for permanent residence as long as:

- you continue to meet the requirements of the Rules for United Kingdom Ancestry
- you have spent a period of four years in employment in the UK in this way, without a break.

An application for permanent residence is made to the Immigration and Nationality Directorate (IND).

Can my family join me in the UK?

Your husband, wife, or eligible partner and children under 18 years of age can join you in the UK if:

- they have a visa for this purpose
- you can support them and live without any help from public funds.

VISITOR VISA

How do I qualify to travel to the UK as a visitor?

You must be able to prove that:

- you want to visit the UK for no more than six months
- you intend to leave the UK at the end of your visit
- you have enough money to support yourself and live in the UK without working or assistance from public funds.

You will need to obtain a visa to visit the UK if you:

- are from a Visa National Country (this information can be found on www.ukvisas.gov.uk)
- are stateless (you do not have a nationality)
- hold a non-national travel document (a travel document which does not give you the nationality of the country that issued it)
- hold a passport issued by an authority that is not recognised in the UK.

What am I allowed to do within my time as a visitor?

As a visitor, you can:

- go to meetings and trade fairs, buy goods, and negotiate and complete contracts with UK businesses
- go to conferences and seminars as a delegate
- find out about, check the details of or examine goods
- get training as long as it is classroom-based instruction or limited to observation only.

In limited circumstances you can also enter the UK as a visitor if you are:

- delivering goods from abroad
- a representative of a foreign company coming to service, repair or install their products
- an adviser, consultant, trainer or other kind of specialist who is employed abroad either directly or under contract by the same company or group of companies
- a guest speaker or expert speaker at a conference or seminar or you are running a conference or seminar for no more than five days
- a sportsperson or entertainer travelling for trials, auditions or personal appearances that do not involve performances.

You cannot:

- take paid or unpaid work
- produce goods or provide services in the UK
- sell goods and services to members of the public.

Can I study in the UK?

Yes, as a visitor, you can study during your stay.

Can I get married or register a civil partnership in the UK?

If either you or your future spouse or proposed civil partner are not an EEA national you can visit the UK together to get married or register a civil partnership as long as you intend to leave the country within six months.

Can I get medical treatment in the UK?

Yes. You can apply for a visitor visa to travel to the UK for private medical treatment as long as you can prove that you:

- have made suitable arrangements for the necessary consultation or treatment
- have enough money to pay for the treatment
- have enough money to support yourself and live without working or assistance from public funds while you are in the UK
- intend to leave the UK at the end of your treatment.

ENTRY CLEARANCE

The visas detailed above require citizens of all Visa National Countries and those of any other country who wish to enter the UK for more than six months to make an application for entry clearance prior to travelling to the UK.

There are two types of application which are relevant to the categories covered: non-settlement and settlement. The following information will give you a better understanding of this process and should answer any questions you may have.

How do I apply for a visa?

You are required to complete a visa application form. If you are applying for a non-settlement visa this is VAF1 – non-settlement form; if you are applying for a settlement visa this is the VAF2 – settlement form. These forms can be obtained from any British Mission overseas or can be downloaded at www.ukvisas.gov.uk. There is no charge for these forms. You should apply for a visa in the country of which you are a national or where you legally live.

You can apply in a number of ways: by post, by courier, in person and online. The visa section of the British Mission in the country where you need to apply will advise which of these options are available.

What do I need to make my application?

You will need to supply the following:

- correctly completed VAF1 – non-settlement application form, or VAF2 – settlement application form
- your passport or travel document.
- a recent passport-sized (45mm x 35mm) colour photograph of yourself, which should be:
  - taken against a light-coloured background
  - clear and of good quality, and not framed or backed
  - printed on normal photographic paper
  - full face and without sunglasses, hat or other head covering unless you wear this for cultural or religious reasons
- the visa fee; this cannot be refunded, and you must normally pay it in the local currency of the country where you are applying
- any relevant supporting documents.

What supporting documents should I include with my application?

You should include all the documents you can to show that you qualify for entry to the UK in the category in which you are applying.

What happens when I make my application?

The entry clearance officer will try to make a decision using your application form and the supporting documents you have provided. If this is not possible, they will need to interview you.

If your application is successful, you will be issued with a visa. It is imperative that you check this to make sure that:

- your personal details are correct
- it correctly states the purpose for which you want to come to the UK
- it is valid for the date on which you want to travel (you can ask for it to be post-dated for up to three months if you do not plan to travel immediately).

If you think there is anything wrong with your visa, you must contact the visa section that processed your application immediately.

INDEFINITE LEAVE TO REMAIN (ILR)

Full or permanent residency is properly known as Indefinite Leave to Remain. You are able to apply for this in several ways depending on your UK immigration status at the time of application.

Indefinite Leave to Remain allows the holder to remain in the UK for an indefinite period, on the condition that he/she intends to remain present and settled. If you have been granted Indefinite Leave to Remain and leave the UK for a period of two years or more, it is usually deemed that you are not present and settled and therefore your ILR status will be revoked.

Indefinite Leave to Remain allows the holder to work without restriction in the UK. It also allows exit and re-entry on multiple occasions.

The following are some ways in which an individual may apply for Indefinite Leave to Remain:

- shortly before the expiry of a two-year marriage visa
- on the basis of being married to or in a relationship for four years or more with a British citizen or a person who has no time limitation of their ability to stay in the UK
- shortly before the expiry of a five-year ancestry visa
- once having held a work permit for a five-year period
- once having legally spent ten years in the UK
- once having spent 14 years in the UK
- once having spent five continuous years as a representative of an overseas newspaper, news agency or broadcasting organisation
- once having spent five years in the UK as a sole representative
- once having spent five years in the UK as an overseas government employee or servant in a diplomatic household
- once having spent five years in the UK as a minister of religion, missionary or member of a religious order
- once having spent a continuous five-year period in the UK as a member of operational ground staff of an overseas-owned airline
- once having spent a continuous five-year period in the UK as a person established in business under the provisions of the EU Association Agreement
- once having spent a continuous five years in the UK as an investor or retired person of independent means
- once having spent a continuous five years in the UK as a writer, composer or artist.

An EEA national and the family members of this person may apply for ILR if they have been issued a residence permit or document for five years. They must have remained, and intend to continue to do so, in the UK for at least four years.

LONG RESIDENCY VISA

The long residency visa is divided into two types – the ten-year visa and the 14-year visa.

The ten-year visa may be considered if the applicant has been legally resident in the UK with Home Office approval for ten years. Usually, if successful, the applicant will be allowed to the remain in the UK without time limitation, and granted Indefinite Leave To Remain (ILR).

The 14-year visa may be considered if the applicant has been resident in the UK for more than 14 years legally or illegally. Again this will normally qualify the applicant for Indefinite Leave to Remain status as it will be deemed that he/she considers the UK to be their home. This type of application will be considered as long as there are no strong countering issues, such as a criminal record.

There is also the ability to apply for a visa after seven years. This may be considered if a person has remained in the UK for more than seven years where that person is facing removal from the UK and he/she has young children with them in the UK who have also resided in the UK for more than seven years.

10

Registration as a British citizen

Certain persons born between 1961 and 1983 to mothers who were citizens of the United Kingdom and Colonies at the time of their birth may apply for registration as a British citizen. An applicant is entitled to registration if he/she:

- was born after 7 February 1961 but before 1 January 1983
- was born to a mother who was a citizen of the United Kingdom and Colonies at the time of birth and had it been possible for women to pass on citizenship of the UK to their children in the same way as men could, would have been a citizen of the United Kingdom and Colonies by descent
- had been a citizen of the United Kingdom and Colonies, would have had the right of abode in the UK and would have become a British citizen on 1 January 1983.

An applicant will meet the second requirement if at the time of birth:

a) their mother was a citizen of the United Kingdom and Colonies either:

   - by birth, legal adoption, naturalisation or registration in the United Kingdom and Colonies; or
   - by birth, before 1 January 1949, in a British protectorate, protected state or United Kingdom trust territory; or

b) their mother was, at the time of their birth, a citizen of the United Kingdom and Colonies and:

   (i) the applicant was born, or their mother was born, in a British protectorate, protected state, mandated territory or trust territory or in any foreign place in which British subjects came under British extraterritorial jurisdiction; or
   (ii) the applicant was born in a non-Commonwealth country and his/her birth was registered, within one year of its occurrence, at a British consulate;
   (iii) the applicant's mother was in Crown service under the United Kingdom government at the time of his/her birth; or
   (iv) the applicant was born in a Commonwealth country whose citizenship law had been the subject of an order under section 32(8) of the British Nationality Act 1948, but did not become a citizen of that country at birth.

The third requirement is met if:

(i) the applicant's mother was, at the time of his/her birth, a citizen of the United Kingdom and Colonies by birth, legal adoption, naturalisation or registration (except registration on the basis of a marriage on or after 28 October 1971 to a citizen of the United Kingdom and Colonies) in the United Kingdom, Channel Islands or Isle of Man; or
(ii) one of the applicant's mother's parents (the definition of 'parent' here excludes the father, but includes the mother, of an illegitimate child) was a citizen of the United Kingdom and Colonies in the way mentioned in (i) above at the time of her birth; or

(iii) the applicant was settled in the United Kingdom before 1983 and had, at that time, been ordinarily resident there for the last 5 years or more; or

(iv) the applicant is a woman who, before 1 January 1983, was or had been married to man with the right of abode in the United Kingdom.

A successful applicant will become a British citizen by descent. As a British citizen by descent you will not normally be able to pass on British citizenship to any children born outside British territory.

11

Proposed migration policy

A new points-based system to enable the UK to control migration more effectively, tackle abuse and identify the most talented workers was launched by the Home Secretary on 7 March 2006.

Unveiling the government's Command Paper on the points-based system for managed migration, the Home Secretary called on industry and education sectors to play their role in making migration work for Britain, and reminded them that they had a responsibility to help make the new scheme a success.

The points-based system is a central part of the government's five-year strategy for asylum and immigration, which was published in February 2005, and is committed to a wide-ranging plan: to ensure that only those who benefit Britain can come here to work or study; to strengthen the UK's borders; to crack down on abuse and illegal immigration; and increase removals. Its implementation is a key government priority.

The scheme will be complemented with a tougher approach from British embassies abroad to weed out false applications and will place increased obligations on UK businesses and universities who will now be required to sponsor migrants and help to ensure that those they sponsor adhere to the terms of their visa.

Key elements of the system include the following.

1. Consolidating more than 80 existing work and study routes into five tiers:

   Tier 1 – highly skilled, e.g. scientists or entrepreneurs
   Tier 2 – skilled workers with a job offer, e.g. nurses, teachers, engineers
   Tier 3 – low skilled workers filling specific temporary labour shortages, e.g. construction workers for a particular project
   Tier 4 – students
   Tier 5 – youth mobility and temporary workers, e.g. working holidaymakers or musicians coming to play a concert.

   - Points to be awarded will reflect aptitude, experience, age and also the level of need in any given sector, to allow the UK to respond flexibly to changes in the labour market.
   - The establishment of a Skills Advisory Body to identify these shortages.
   - Consolidating entry clearance and work permit applications into one transparent, single-stage application.

2. A system of sponsorship by employers and educational institutions to ensure compliance.

3. Financial securities for specific categories where there has been evidence of abuse to ensure that migrants return home at the end of their stay.

4. The ending of employment routes to the UK for low-skilled workers from outside the EU except in cases of short-term shortages.

The Home Secretary said:

> Managed migration is in the interest of the UK. Today's

> announcement sets out the government's policy to deliver a firm but fair, simpler, more transparent and more rigorous system, which will benefit our economy and protect our borders.
>
> Crucially, it will allow us to ensure that only those people with the skills the UK needs come to this country while preventing those without these skills applying. Foreign workers or students will also in future need a UK sponsor to vouch for them, ensuring that businesses and colleges take responsibility for making sure foreign workers and students comply with visa rules.
>
> This new scheme fits alongside other activity being undertaken to tighten up our immigration procedures. We are implementing new technology through the e-borders programme to record simply and effectively details of passengers intending to enter or leave the UK before they begin their journey, and by the end of 2006 we will begin to require individuals applying for visas to be fingerprinted.

Proposals for a points-based system for managed migration are a key element of the Home Office's five-year strategy for asylum and immigration, *Controlling our Borders: Making Migration Work for Britain* published in February 2005. The government undertook an extensive consultation on the proposals between July and November 2005.

The system aims to ensure that only those migrants who benefit the UK – for example, the highly skilled such as surgeons or scientists or those who are coming to fill gaps in the labour market that cannot be met from the domestic workforce such as teachers and nurses, can come to work or study, while introducing new measures to ensure that migrants comply with their leave to remain and go home at the end of their stay.

The UK will benefit from increased economic and international competitiveness and cultural exchange. Also included in this announcement are decisions by:

- the Department of Health to end the existing immigration routes for postgraduate doctors and dentists, except for those people who have studied for their degrees in the UK; This reflects the flexibility of the managed migration system to ensure the needs of the UK labour market are met
- the Home Office to end existing low-skilled work routes including the Sectors Based Scheme and the Seasonal Agricultural Workers Scheme, again reflecting the fact that labour from the new EU member states is now filling many vacancies in these areas.

The Home Secretary said:

> The publication of the government's policy on managed migration is a step in a process to overhauling the UK's immigration system for workers and students. That work is ongoing and will not take effect overnight. A constructive dialogue has already been established between industry and government, which will continue as the system is put in place.

At the time of going to print specific details had not been released. For further and up-to-date information, we suggest you check our website, www.amblercollins.com or speak to a specialist consultant.

(Crown Copyright, from www.ind.homeoffice,gov.uk)

PART THREE

12

Employment

Finding a job, either full-time or part-time, requires a degree of patience and commitment. It is unlikely that you will be able to pick up your ideal job straight away so ideally you need to begin looking and applying before you leave for the UK.

The economic situation in the UK is sound, which means that finding work should be relatively easy, depending on your skills. The unemployment rate in 2005 was 4.9 per cent. The number of unemployed people was 1.42 million in 2005.

THE MAIN JOB SECTORS AND WHAT YOU CAN EXPECT

Health Services

Nursing

There is a constant demand for nurses in the National Health Service (NHS), private hospitals, clinics, surgeries and nursing homes.

You will need a relevant nursing qualification to work as a nurse in the UK and will also need to register with the Nursing and Midwifery Council (NMC). It's recommended you register with them before you leave for the UK as registration can take a while. But once approved, registration lasts for three years. The NMC charges an application fee then a further fee if you are accepted. You will also need police clearance if you are planning to work with children. All the relevant forms and further details are available from their website www.nmc-uk.org.uk.

Typical working hours:	35–45 hours per week
Typical rates of pay:	£7+ per hour depending on experience and qualifications

Doctors

Doctors are also always in demand, particularly house officers, house surgeons, house physicians, housemen, senior house officers, registrars, specialist registrars and clinical assistants.

All doctors wishing to practise in the UK must hold the relevant qualifications and experience and must register with the General Medical Council (GMC). Doctors are eligible for full registration if they qualified at a UK or European Economic Area (EEA) medical school and are a national of the EEA. If you qualified in New Zealand, Australia or South Africa you will still be eligible to register but you should check with the GMC for further information. Registration forms can be downloaded from the site www.gmc-uk.org.

Typical working hours:	Locums can work 20–100 hours a week
Typical rates of pay:	Locums can earn £14–£20 per hour

A number of hospital locum positions come with free or highly subsidised accommodation.

Dentists

The UK offers a range of locum and permanent posts on a continual basis. As part of the relevant qualifications, you must register with the General Dental Council (GDC) in order to practise in the UK. It is vital that you contact them to register and determine your eligibility before you leave for the UK. All dentists who qualified after December 2000 in a country other than in the EEA will now have to pass a three-stage international qualifying exam in order to work in the UK. Further details can be obtained by visiting www.gdc-uk.org.

Typical working hours: 40–45 hours per week
Typical rates of pay: £18+ in locum positions

Other medical professions

The Health Professions Council (HPC) deals with a whole range of specialist professionals within the health sector. You can find information including contact details for the professional bodies and forms for download at www.hpcuk.org.

Education

Teachers

Positions in the education sector for teachers, deputy heads, and head teachers are available throughout the UK. A full teaching qualification, criminal clearance and recent professional references will be required in order to work.

Typical working hours: The teaching day is usually 08:30–15:30
Typical rates of pay: £115+ per day

IT and telecoms

IT and telecommunications industries still have jobs for skilled and experienced staff and there are hundreds of companies based across the UK to choose from. Positions typically available are database programmers, administrators, helpdesk staff, project managers, technicians and website developers.

Relevant work experience and qualifications are essential. All the big software systems are used: Microsoft Office, Vba, Oracle, Bahn, SAP, C++, SQL, Sybase, as well as web-based programs such as Perl and html.

Typical working hours:	40–60 hours per week
Typical rates of pay:	£12–£50+ depending on age and experience

Finance

Accountancy

London is one of the major finance capitals of the world, so there are plenty of opportunities for accountants and other financial-based staff. Temporary work in this sector is as diverse as the range of permanent opportunities available and therefore typically includes:

- financial control and direction
- management accounting and financial planning
- regulatory – GAAP, IAS, Sarbannes Oxley
- systems implementation and project management
- financial and business analysis and modelling
- payroll and credit control.

To work in this sector you will need relevant qualifications, and previous experience is essential to secure a good position. Computer literacy is essential – especially Excel. Word and Access experience would also open doors to a wider number of project type roles.

Typical working hours:	40–60 hours per week
Typical part qualified accountant:	£10+ per hour
Typical qualified accountant with experience:	£20–£35+ per hour

Banking

Retail banking is very similar to that operated in Australia, New Zealand and South Africa, with similar products and services being offered. In the UK the main high-street banks include HSBC, Barclays, NatWest, HBoS, RBS and LloydsTSB. Typically roles include:

- front office
- accounting and reporting
- managerial positions
- compliance functions
- reconciliations
- call centre staff.

To work in this sector, experience is important. Although the laws, regulations and operations in the UK retail banking may differ from those you have experience of, the banks offer very strong in-house training programmes to bring you up to speed.

Typical working hours:	40–50 hours per week
Typical rates of pay:	£8–£15+ per hour depending on position and seniority

Legal professional

There is a variety of work on offer in the UK at many levels from temporary or contract paralegals to permanent solicitors in all areas of the law, in private practice, local government and in-house legal departments.

Relevant qualifications and a minimum of six months' experience are generally necessary for temporary and paralegal work.

Typical hours of work:	35–40 hours per week
Typical rates of pay:	£9–£20 + per hour

Hospitality and catering

Bar staff

There is still plenty of work for bar staff. While experience is a bonus, all you need is enthusiasm and friendliness.

Working hours: Hours are usually based around working shifts. Some pubs in the City of London don't open on the weekends. New licensing laws in England came into effect in November 2005 and allow 24-hour drinking licences for those premises that have successfully applied. The UK government is also planning that all restaurants and pubs and bars preparing and serving food would be smoke-free and by the end of 2008 these arrangements for licensed premises would be in place.

Rates of pay: up to £5 per hour. This may include some drinks or food. Tipping is not the norm in the UK pubs although it is more common in the trendier bars.

Catering

There are loads of positions available, from chef to waiting staff. Qualifications for the top kitchen jobs will be required and past experience for waiting roles will be useful.

Typical working hours:	Long hours and weekends
Typical pay rates	Commis chef around £12,000 per year

Tradespeople

If you are a qualified tradesperson, such as an electrician, plumber, quantity surveyor, engineer, etc., you should have little difficulty finding work. Training certificates and experience are essential.

Typical hours of work:	40 + hours
Typical rates of pay:	Can vary significantly from area to area according to demand.

WHERE TO FIND WORK

Thinking laterally about how and where you find work could broaden your chances of successfully finding a rewarding and fulfilling job. When searching for employment, it is important to exploit every possible avenue to find the opportunity that will suit you.

Many job vacancies are handled by recruitment companies, but there are also other ways to find work. Depending on the current stage of your career, all or a combination of the job sources below could be useful.

Recruitment agencies

Not all recruitment agencies are equal. When deciding which recruitment agencies to register with, there are a few things you should take into account. Always look for an agency that is established and has a good reputation in the marketplace. Good companies are very choosy about the recruitment agencies they align themselves with and will only want to work with recruiters who attract top talent and have proven success. As a result, these agencies will have a much better and wider range of job opportunities on offer and are more likely to help you progress your career.

Another factor to consider is whether the consultants are working on a commission. Many recruitment consultants rely on commission to make up their salary, which can mean that their advice is not always completely objective. It is not unusual for candidates to be talked into taking a job because it is the end of month and a consultant is down on his or her commission earnings for that month.

Newspapers

Familiarise yourself with those newspapers that cater specifically for your profession and get to know on which days job vacancies are advertised. For example, accountants will use the *Financial Times* and jobs are advertised on Mondays and Thursdays; *The Guardian* advertises media jobs on a Monday. Visit the corresponding websites to further search for jobs and to research company information. Your local newspaper will also have a 'jobs day' and this should be read weekly too. Again, more senior vacancies tend to be advertised nationally or in industry journals rather than regionally, but your local paper will keep you updated with business information specific to your region. The chapter 'Useful information' includes a list of the main media websites.

Avoid regional job magazines which are often merely a tardy repetition of the local paper's jobs pages. Remember that newspapers generally are still a great source for jobs.

Trade magazines/professional journals

If you are a member of a professional body, you should regularly read any relevant magazine, to view advertised vacancies and keep yourself updated with industry information. Many such publications are subscription only and if you are not doing so already, now is the time to purchase your subscription. Students/graduates embarking on a professional career can often take advantage of reduced subscription rates. These publications are a key source in your job search.

The Internet

A key way to search for a job is through the Internet. All of the above mentioned sources, from agencies to newspapers, will have websites on which vacancies can be found. There are also job 'boards' which range from very generalist jobs, with thousands of job listings, to more specialist sites with fewer jobs. Most sites have search facilities that enable you to specify criteria such as discipline, job type, salary, location. Some provide user logins that will save your details and 'post' any relevant jobs to you as they come in.

One of the largest recruitment companies, Michael Page, carries approximately 10,000 UK-based jobs that you can access online and which are updated hourly, with only current, live jobs being advertised (in theory). Their online application process is quick and easy and once you have applied for one job, there is no need to resubmit your CV with subsequent applications. You can also sign up to receive jobs that match your criteria by email. This gives you the advantage of knowing about new job opportunities before other candidates.

Below are some of the most popular online job sites for you to search:

www.totaljobs.com
www.workthing.com
www.scotcareers.co.uk

www.jobsearch.co.uk
www.monster.co.uk
www.michaelpage.co.uk/
www.fish4jobs.co.uk
www.jobswales.co.uk
www.hotjobs.yahoo.com/
www.jobcentreplus.gov.uk
www.reed.co.uk/
www.londonofficejobs.co.uk/
www.londonjobs.co.uk/
www.topjobs.co.uk/net/HomePage.aspx
www.jobsite.co.uk/
www.jobs1.co.uk/
www.jobs.nhs.uk/
www.mediplacements.com
www.e-cvs.net/top30.asp

One of the quality weekly newspapers in the UK, the *Sunday Times*, runs a special 'Top 100 companies to work for' list once a year. Go to www.timesonline.co.uk to see who's included on the latest list.

Approaching companies directly

If approached correctly, direct speculative applications can sometimes uncover vacancies. It is sensible to find the relevant recruitment contact within the organisation and address any application to them. Do not bombard them with follow-up calls and letters. Take no for an answer and be prepared in some cases not to receive a reply at all, if no vacancy has been advertised. Ensure that your cover letter clearly states the type of job you are interested in and ensure it is something you are realistically suitable for.

On a similar note, do not be afraid to ask friends, colleagues and family whether their employers are recruiting. Many companies today actively encourage employees to introduce prospective candidates to their business, in some cases awarding cash 'bounties' if an individual is sourced and recruited this way.

Job centres

No matter what your opinion is of job centres, they are packed with job vacancies which are updated daily. Advisers are on hand to arrange interviews where appropriate. There are obviously far fewer opportunities advertised via this source for professionals but if you are at the more junior stages of your career, these centres can be helpful.

Internal company transfer

If you already work for an overseas business with UK offices, you may be able to transfer within your existing company. You will need to speak with your human resources or personnel department to determine if and how this could be done.

Get yourself updated

If, despite your best efforts, you are finding the job market slow, now may be an ideal opportunity to bring any rusty skills up to date or indeed embark on a course/qualification that will be helpful to your job search. If you are considering this, visit http://www.hero.ac.uk/, which lists all universities and colleges of higher and further education in the UK. It provides useful links into websites and is a short cut to any local education information you need.

APPLYING FOR JOBS

CVs are called a variety of things (e.g., curriculum vitae, resumé). There is no universally accepted format. The most important attribute of a successful CV is that it clearly explains to the reader what it is that you can do for them. As a quick guide, your CV should be:

- a well-presented, selling document
- a source of interesting, relevant information
- a script for talking about yourself.

The purpose of your CV is not to get you the job. Its purpose is to get you an interview, and after your meeting to remind the person you met with about you. Remember – you are not writing a CV for yourself, you are writing it for the reader. So, as you write your CV, put yourself in the shoes of the intended reader.

13

How to write the perfect CV and cover letter

More often than not, your CV is the first impression that you'll make on a potential employer. Here's how to present yourself clearly and professionally.

It is worth remembering that each recruiter's idea of a 'perfect' CV will be slightly different. Nonetheless, your CV will in most cases be the first impression an employer has of you. Indeed a strong CV can occasionally itself secure you a job, especially if you are applying for temporary work. At worst, a poorly constructed CV can give a potential employer a negative impression of you as a candidate and bar you from securing that all-important interview.

Taking a little time on design, construction and wording and using the following guidelines to write and submit your CV, will ensure you promote yourself to your best advantage.

CV STRUCTURE

Start with your personal details: full name, date of birth and contact details including all usable telephone numbers. Avoid superfluous details such as religious affiliation, children's names, etc.

Educational history and professional qualifications should follow, including names of institutions and dates attended in reverse order – university before school results. List grades and passes attained.

(These details will matter more if you have recently entered the job market than if, for example, you left full-time education 20 years ago). Include computer skills and (genuine) foreign language skills and any other recent training/development that is relevant to the role applied for.

The most widely accepted style of employment record is the chronological CV. Career history is presented in reverse date order starting with the most recent. Achievements and responsibilities should be listed against each role. More emphasis/information should be put on more recent jobs.

A functional CV can sometimes be more appropriate, for example if you have held a number of unrelated jobs. This presentation would emphasise key skills which can be grouped together under suitable headings. However, career progression and the nature of jobs held can be unclear with this type of CV.

Leave hobbies and interests to last – keep this section short. References can simply be 'available on request'. Current salary details should not be included. A good cover letter should always accompany your CV.

Your CV and cover letter should combine to create a picture of you and your career to date and illustrate why you are different from the competition. With this successfully achieved (and a bit of luck!), you will secure yourself a place on a shortlist.

GENERAL TIPS

- Your CV should be laser-printed in black ink using a plain typeface, on good-quality A4 white/cream paper.

- Decorative borders are not necessary, nor are photographs of you.
- If applying by post, your CV and cover letter should be submitted in a suitable quality envelope, clearly addressed, with a first-class stamp. If applying by email, time should be taken designing and formatting to ensure your details read clearly. Send a copy to yourself to check before submitting it for a role.
- Your CV should ideally cover no more than two pages and never more than three. Aim to ensure the content is clear, structured, concise and relevant. Using bullet points rather than full sentences can help minimise word usage.
- A basic CV may need tailoring with each job application to best suit the requirements of the role applied for.
- The completed CV needs to be checked carefully for grammatical errors and spelling mistakes – which always leave a poor impression – and to ensure that it makes sense. Ask an 'independent' party to review the whole document before it is put into use.
- Remember when writing and structuring your CV that it is essentially a marketing document on you and that a potential employer will use the details provided to form interview questions. It should be clear and easy to read. Gaps in career history should be explained and falsehoods and inaccuracies avoided.
- There is no reason to include your reasons for leaving each job on your CV but be prepared to answer such questions in your interview.

EFFECTIVE CVS – A STANDARD TWO-PAGE PRINTED CV

The decision to recruit is like a buying decision on the part of an employer. Your CV must:

- meet the needs of the target organisation where possible; this means a single generalist CV is unlikely to be sufficient
- highlight your achievements and how they relate to the job you are applying for; it must give the reader a clear indication of why you should be considered for this role.

To decide what to include in your CV and where, follow these principles and guidelines:

- Generally, the document should contain no more than two pages. Sometimes, a one-page summary is all that is required.
- Your CV should be honest and factual.
- The first page should contain enough personal details for a recruitment consultant or potential employer to contact you easily.
- Choose a presentation format that allows you to headline key skills, key achievements or key attributes.
- Your employment history should commence with your current or most recent job and work backwards.
- Achievements should be short, bullet-pointed statements and include your role, the action you took and a comment on the result of your action.

- Where information clearly demonstrates your suitability for the vacancy you're applying for, and enhances your chances of being shortlisted, include this information near the beginning of the CV.

- Leave out information that is irrelevant or negative.

- Include details of recent training or skills development events you have attended which could be relevant.

- List all your professional memberships and relevant qualifications.

The most common contents of a CV include:

- personal details
- skills and career summary (as an introduction)
- key achievements
- qualifications
- career history.

Don't forget: the ultimate test of your CV is whether it meets the needs of the person making the buying decision, and whether you feel comfortable with its content and style.

When you submit a printed CV to a recruiter or a potential employer, it is likely to be the first thing they get to see or read of yours. Therefore, you need to present your CV well and make it user-friendly. Observe the following guidelines:

- Use a good-quality paper, typically 100gsm in weight and watermarked. In most cases, be conservative and print your CV in black ink on white paper. Covering letters should use identical stationery.

- Lay out your CV neatly.
- Don't make the margins too deep or too narrow.
- Resist writing lengthy paragraphs – be concise.
- Careful use of bold type can be effective.
- Typefaces such as Times New Roman or Arial are fairly standard.
- Do not use a type size less than 11pt.
- Check for spelling or typographical errors – whoever actually types your CV, errors are your responsibility. Don't rely on a spell checker. If you're not sure about a word, resort to a dictionary. Sloppiness and lack of care could be heavily penalised.

Key skills/competencies/attributes

Summarise the things about you that are relevant to this role. You can present the information as a list of achievements, a summary of skills, or a list of key competencies (this choice should be made in consultation with your career consultant). Give as much evidence as you can to suggest that you are suited to the career that you are pursuing.

HOW TO WRITE THE PERFECT COVER LETTER

A good covering letter can differentiate your CV from the countless others that pass across employers' desks.

When responding to an advertised job vacancy, whether via letter, email or fax, you should always include a covering letter with your CV. Treat it as a vital part of your personal marketing literature, which merits attention and consideration. A cover letter introduces you and your CV and is your first chance to make a good impression on your potential employer. Aim to make it entice the reader to take those few extra minutes to consider you against other applicants. Your CV should not be sent without one.

You should write a cover letter as a personalised document. However, here are some basic guidelines that should help ensure you receive a positive response from your initial contact.

Appearance and layout

Handwritten or typed cover letters can be equally acceptable and opinion is still divided on this issue. However, increasingly recruiters are asking that applicants email their details, leaving the hand-written posted option a non-starter. Whatever the method of your application, ensure your letter is neatly and clearly presented on paper of a similar size and quality to your CV. Check and check again for grammatical and spelling errors. Handwriting should be neat and legible. Emails should be written in a common font with standard formatting. They should emulate a handwritten letter in terms of style.

Your letter should address the relevant contact; the name of the contact often appears in the job advert. Avoid 'Sir or Madam' if possible. Unlike a CV, it is acceptable to write a cover letter in the first person.

Content

The content of your cover letter should be brief and structured, avoiding lengthy repetition of information covered in your CV. Firstly, clarify your approach. If you are replying to an advert, say so. Mention job title, any reference number and where and when you saw it.

NAME
Address
Telephone

A Customer Service Centre Manager with 17 years broad experience within XYZ Bank. Recent responsibilities and achievements have been concerned with managing 22 staff to provide a high quality service handling all back-office functions and customer enquiries for 25 retail branches. Previously responsible for ensuring the provision of an efficient counter service within retail branches and the associated staff training and development.

CAREER HISTORY

1983 – 2003 XYZ BANK PLC

A major clearing bank providing a full range of retail banking and insurance products and services. Employees c. 10,000.

1995 – 2003 Manager, Customer Service Centre, Farnham

The Customer Service Centre was established in 1990, being one of 45 set up throughout the country. Its primary purpose is to provide an administration and support function to 25 retail branches within Surrey.

This involves the handling of all routine back-office functions, such as documentation, telephone answering, cheque dealing, regular payments and responding to customer enquiries and requests for services.

Reported to the Regional Customer Service Centre Director with responsibilities for management, training and development of typically 25 staff and monitoring the quality of the total service provided.

ACHIEVEMENTS

- ☐ Customer service standard target for 1994/95 was 99%. Performance achieved by Centre 99.20%. Annual telephone performance for 1994/95 achieved 99.77% against target of 95%. The measures monitor Centre performance in respect of timeliness, responsiveness, accuracy and control.
- ☐ Introduced the resource management system at the Centre enabling the forecasting of work volumes to be matched to resources available, which resulted in increased productivity, i.e. staff numbers have reduced over a six-month period from 22 to 19 but productivity has been maintained at same level.
- ☐ Launched a staff attitude survey at the Centre in 1997. Action plan produced by local team to address issues raised. Resulted in improvement to communication within the Centre by changing format/frequency of team meetings.

Examples of typical CV content and layouts
Example 1

- ☐ Implemented the customer care programme to provide a quality telephone service to our customers; success measured in feedback received from branches and from 'Mystery Shopper' survey.

1993 – 1995 Assistant Manager, Customer Service Centre, Farnham

Reported to the Centre Manager with responsibility for the staff resources encompassing work schedules, time records and ensuring that all internal controls were implemented so that work was completed to high standard of accuracy in accordance with Bank procedures.

Conducted formal performance reviews of all direct reports and monitored the reviews of their staff to ensure standards were maintained.

ACHIEVEMENTS

- ☐ Inspection of Centre conducted by auditors in 1994. Achieved score of 89% – standard being 80%.
- ☐ Involved in establishment of Centre from Day One. Worked in conjunction with Manager in organising work areas to ensure effectiveness of Centre.

1986 – 1993 Branch Supervisor, Basingstoke

Reported to the Assistant Manager with responsibility for organising the branch to provide an excellent counter service to customers. Specifically undertook interviews for account opening and initial marketing.

Undertook training and development of staff to ensure their full competency in cashiering duties and was personally responsible for the balancing of tills and reconciliation of internal accounts.

1979 – 1986 Cashier, Various Branches

Reported to the Senior Cashier with general responsibilities for providing an excellent service to customers via both the counter and telephone.

Additionally accountable for balancing the till each day and being up-to-date with current bank products in order to assist with customer enquiries.

EDUCATION

1974 – 1979 Lowlands Comprehensive, Norwich 5 'O' Levels

LEISURE ACTIVITIES

Active exercise, cooking, gardening

Curriculum Vitae

NAME:	Name and Surname
ADDRESS:	Street Name and Number Town/City Postcode/Zipcode
TELEPHONE:	Work/Home Number Mobile Number
EMAIL ADDRESS:	youremail@yahoo.com
DATE OF BIRTH:	Date/Month/Year: dd/mm/yyyy format
STATUS:	Single, Married, Widow, etc.
NATIONALITY:	British, Australian, etc.
VISA:	Visa Status e.g. Ancestry Visa, etc. Start Date of Visa: dd/mm/yyyy format
RELOCATE:	Yes/No
CANDIDATE PROFILE:	Yes/No
EDUCATION:	Start Year – End Year, Name of University Degree Attained Start Year – End Year, Name of School Number of 'O' Levels Number of 'A' Levels A Level and Pass Level A Level and Pass Level A Level and Pass Level
PROFESSIONAL QUALIFICATIONS:	CIMA, ASP Programmer, etc.
LANGUAGES:	Conversational French, etc.
CURRENT EMPLOYER:	ABC Frozen Foods Ltd
CURRENT POSITION:	HR Manager, Accountant, etc.
BASIC SALARY:	Current gross annual salary
BENEFITS PACKAGE:	Bonus, Private Health, Gym, etc.
NOTICE PERIOD:	E.g. 1 calendar month
COMPUTER SKILLS:	Microsoft Word, Excel, etc.

Example 2

WORK EXPERIENCE: Begin with the most recent first

Jan 2001 – Present Company Name

Brief description of company, turnover, and what the company specialise/ specialised in...

Position Held:

Reporting level of the position and a brief description of the role, influence of the role to the business, etc.

Outline of Responsibilities:
- Specific tasks which were required directly by the business, etc.
- Where your role influenced business decisions, direction, etc.
- Examples which showed your personal initiative, self-starter aptitude, etc.
- Tasks which involved team management, motivation, etc.
- Further responsibilities, etc. ...

Specific Project Work/Achievements:

- Successful projects you directed and their direct impact to the business, etc.
- Initiatives you implemented, etc.
- Direct improvements to the business as directed by yourself, etc.
- Further achievements, etc.

Jan 2000 – Dec 2000 Company Name

Brief description of company, turnover, and what the company specialise/ specialised in...

Position Held:

Reporting level of the position and a brief description of the role, influence of the role to the business, etc.

Outline of Responsibilities:
- xx

Jan 1999 – Dec 1999 Company Name

Brief description of company, turnover, and what the company specialise/ specialised in..

Position Held:

Reporting level of the position and a brief description of the role, influence of the role to the business, etc.

Outline of Responsibilities:
- xx

In some cases an advert will indicate that a more substantial letter is required. Always follow a specific instruction and include any information if it is particularly requested, for example, current salary.

Briefly outline your current situation and why you are seeking change. Include current or last job, qualifications and professional and academic training, tailoring your information to make it as relevant as possible to the organisation or job applied for.

Tell the potential employer a little about themselves to demonstrate you have properly read the advert and that you have done some research into the organisation. State why you are interested in them as an employer.

You need to emphasise why an employer may want to meet and employ you. Highlight your transferable skills, achievements and versatility; what you can contribute and what makes you different. Mention personality traits relevant to the role applied for, taking care not to appear too subjective. Ensure the letter flows freely and do not match every point on the job description with an answer. The reader should be left with an overall impression that you are a potentially valuable addition to the workforce.

Negative information of any sort should be avoided in your cover letter as well as CV.

Close your letter politely mentioning that you would like the opportunity to discuss your suitability with them at an interview and that you await a response in due course.

14

Before you go for interview

HOW TO RESEARCH COMPANIES

Before going to your interview, make sure you prepare yourself by finding as much as you can about the hiring organisation. There are numerous sources of information about nearly every company. Information is on the Internet, in the library, in shops, in databases and available from the recruitment company (if the job has been sourced through an agency).

In particular, the Internet should give you a wealth of information about the company and the industry in which the company operates. Most industries also have trade publications so have a read through these to gain knowledge about the industry and current trends and issues that they face.

Here are some tips:

- Call the company/agency and request sales literature, annual reports, technical information, product brochures, information, etc.
- Log on to the Internet and visit the company website, spending time looking at financial information and gaining a good understanding of what the company does, and their goals and values.
- If available, also access the press area of the website. This will give you articles from the media and insightful information about

the company. It will also ensure you are aware of recent press releases involving the company.

- If the company website does not have a press area, access information online through search engines such as Google or MSN. Alternatively, log on to media sites such as the *Financial Times* website and run a search on the company.

PRE-INTERVIEW PLANNING

Research shows that people make their mind up about someone in the first few seconds of meeting with them. So it's best to get off to a good start.

No matter how well qualified you may seem 'on paper' for a job, when recruiting, an employer will still be interested in your personality and presentation. Indeed with more than one suitable applicant for a role, interview performance is often the deciding factor. This makes the face-to-face meeting a critical part of the recruitment process and you will need to impress from the start.

Following the interview preparation guidelines below will help overcome any interview nerves and instil confidence for a productive meeting with your potential employer.

Practical tips

- Double-check the date, time and location of the interview and be familiar with the name and title of the interviewer. Take your interview confirmation letter with you.

- Prepare your interview outfit in advance. Ensure your appearance is both smart and comfortable.

- Familiarise yourself with the journey to the location, to ensure you arrive in plenty of time. If driving, do a 'dummy run'. Check timetables and book train tickets in advance. Anticipate delays, especially on unknown routes. Contact your interviewer swiftly if you are unavoidably delayed on the day.
- Do not arrive over-laden with belongings. Take any requested certificates, references, etc., a spare CV and a notepad and pen. A mobile phone is always useful, but ensure it is turned off before arrival.
- Be punctual for your meeting but it is inadvisable to arrive more than half an hour early. Leave yourself enough time to visit the toilets and tidy up if necessary.
- Remember that you start making an impression on your prospective employer the moment you arrive at reception. Be courteous to the receptionist and any other staff you may meet prior to your interview. Their opinion of you is often sought and may even have some influence on the final selection.

15

Attending the interview

DRESS TO IMPRESS

If you are going for an interview it is customary to 'dress to impress' – which means a business suit, shirt and tie for men and business suit for women. First impressions are very important if you want to land the job, so be smart and professional.

BODY LANGUAGE

When you attend an interview be aware of your body language, as the interviewer will be. Look relaxed but not too laid back; be attentive, giving good eye contact to your interviewer, and look and appear professional in how you stand, shake hands and reply to their questions. Don't put other employers down and don't be over-confident. If you appear fidgety, slouchy or are paying more attention to what's happening around you it is unlikely you will project the right impression, regardless of your answers to the interviewers' questions.

REFERENCES

It is standard practice for employers to ask for references – normally two, but sometimes three. The first should be an academic referee; usually your supervisor, but you could use the head or another member of the department. The other is a personal referee, someone (not a relative) who knows you as an individual; a family friend, a neighbour or perhaps a former employer who could comment on you as an employee as well. Don't name referees without first consulting them to seek their permission. You should also advise them on what you are applying for. Consider briefing them on what the job involves and what the employer is looking for. Make sure they have relevant information about you. It is also a good idea to keep referees informed on your progress. Give their full title (e.g. Professor, Dr.), status (e.g. Head of Department, Warden) and their correct address including the postcode.

SOME OTHER USEFUL TIPS

- Greet your interviewer standing, with a strong, firm handshake and a smile. Good body language is vital. Sit up straight with both feet on the floor. Speak clearly and confidently. Try to maintain a comfortable level of eye contact throughout.

- A standard interview will generally start with an introductory chat, moving on to questions specific to your application and experience. General information about the company and role may follow, finishing with an opportunity for you to ask your own questions.

- Be familiar with your CV and prepared to answer questions from it. Similarly, ensure you have read any job description thoroughly and think of ways in which your experience will benefit your potential employer.

- Listen to what is being asked of you. Think about your answers to more difficult questions and do not give irrelevant detail. Give positive examples from your experience to date but be concise. Avoid one-word answers. Prepare yourself in advance for likely questions (see below for common interview questions).

- Be ready to ask questions that you have prepared beforehand. This can demonstrate that you have thought about the role and done some research on the organisation. Ensure they are open questions, thus encouraging the interviewer to provide you with additional information.

- Show your enthusiasm for the role, even if you have some reservations. These can be discussed at a later stage.

TOP TEN INTERVIEW QUESTIONS – AND HOW YOU SHOULD ANSWER THEM

As the saying goes, 'If you fail to plan, you plan to fail'. So here is a valuable insight into the world of interview questions and the techniques best used to answer them.

There are some questions that are asked frequently in interviews and you should prepare your answers beforehand. The key things to remember when responding to interview questions are to keep your answers relevant, brief and to the point. If you are faced with a difficult question, make sure you stay calm, don't get defensive, and take a moment to think about your response before you answer.

Remember, these responses are only suggestions. Try to personalise your response as much as possible.

Q1. *Tell me about yourself.*

A1. Identify some of your main attributes and memorise them. Describe your qualifications, career history and range of skills, emphasising those skills relevant to the job on offer.

Q2. *What have your achievements been to date?*

A2. Select an achievement that is work-related and fairly recent. Identify the skills you used in the achievement and quantify the benefit it had to the company. For example, 'my greatest achievement has been to design and implement a new sales ledger system, bringing it in ahead of time and improving our debtors' position significantly, saving the company £50,000 per month in interest'.

Q3. *Are you happy with your career to date?*

A3. This question is really about your self-esteem, confidence and career aspirations. The answer must be 'yes', followed by a brief explanation as to what it is about your career so far that's made you happy. If you have hit a career plateau, or you feel you are moving too slowly, then you must qualify your answer.

Q4. *What is the most difficult situation you have had to face and how did you tackle it?*

A4. The purpose of this question is to find out what your definition of 'difficult' is and whether you can show a logical approach to problem-solving. In order to show yourself in a positive light, select a difficult work situation which was not caused by you and which can be quickly explained in a few sentences. Explain how you defined the problem, what the options were, why you selected the one you did and what the outcome was. Always end on a positive note.

Q5. *What do you like about your present job?*

A5. This is a straightforward question. All you have to do is make sure that your 'likes' correspond to the skills, etc., required in the job on offer. Be enthusiastic; describe your job as interesting and diverse but do not overdo it – after all, you are looking to leave.

Q6. *What do you dislike about your present job?*

A6. Be cautious with this answer. Do not be too specific as you may draw attention to weaknesses that will leave you open to further problems. One approach is to choose a characteristic of your present company, such as its size or slow decision-making processes, etc. Give your answer with the air of someone who takes problems and frustrations in your stride as part of the job.

Q7. *What are your strengths?*

A7. This is one question that you know you are going to get, so there is no excuse for being unprepared. Concentrate on discussing your main strengths. List three or four proficiencies, e.g. your ability to learn quickly, determination to succeed, positive attitude, your ability to relate to people and achieve a common goal. You may be asked to give examples of the above so be prepared.

Q8. *What is your greatest weakness?*

A8. Do not say you have none – this will lead to further problems. You have two options – use a professed weakness such as a lack of experience (not ability) on your part in an area that is not vital for the job. The second option is to describe a personal or professional weakness that could also be considered to be a strength, and the steps you have taken to combat it. An example would be, 'I know my team thinks I'm too demanding at times – I tend to drive them pretty hard but I'm getting much better at using the carrot and not the stick'.

Q9. *Why do you want to leave your current employer?*

A9. State how you are looking for a new challenge, more responsibility, experience and a change of environment. Do not be negative in your reasons for leaving. It is rarely appropriate to cite salary as your primary motivator.

Q10. *Why have you applied for this particular job?*

A10. The employer is looking for evidence that the job suits you, fits in with your general aptitudes, coincides with your long-term goals and involves doing things you enjoy. Make sure you have a good understanding of the role and the organisation, and describe the attributes of the organisation that interest you most.

OTHER QUESTIONS AN EMPLOYER MAY ASK

- How does your job fit in to your department and company?
- What do you enjoy about this industry?
- Give an example of when you have worked under pressure.
- What kinds of people do you like working with?
- Give me an example of when your work was criticised.
- Give me an example of when you have felt anger at work. How did you cope and did you still perform a good job?
- What kind of people do you find it difficult to work with?
- Give me an example of when you have had to face a conflict of interest at work.
- Tell me about the last time you disagreed with your boss.
- Give me an example of when you haven't got on with others.
- Do you prefer to work alone or in a group? Why?
- This organisation is very different to your current employer – how do you think you are going to fit in?
- What are you looking for in a company?
- How do you measure your own performance?
- What kind of pressures have you encountered at work?
- Are you a self-starter? Give me examples to demonstrate this.
- What changes in the workplace have caused you difficulty and why?
- How do you feel about working long hours and/or weekends?
- Give me an example of when you have been out of your depth.
- What have you failed to achieve to date?
- What can you bring to this organisation?

16

Attending assessment centres

Some employers combine the classic interview with other techniques such as activities at assessment centres. So, if a day full of role plays, group exercises, behavioural interviews, verbal and numerical testing, presentations and psychometric tests is your idea of hell – read on.

WHAT TO EXPECT FROM AN ASSESSMENT CENTRE

If you are invited to an assessment centre you can be sure that you have done something right and the employer is keen to see what else you are capable of. It can be daunting but is only those who have passed through the preliminary interviews and those that the employer thinks are capable of successfully carrying out the jobs on offer that are asked to attend – so be confident and positive.

Assessment centres are designed to test your intellectual capabilities and future potential. The employer will set tasks aimed at testing your strengths and uncovering your weaknesses. In turn, you will learn more about the company, how it motivates its personnel, and you will meet some of the people you will work with should you be offered a job.

Assessment centres differ greatly in design, and they may be held at the company's HQ, a hotel or in a rural setting. The form in which the assessment centre comes will reflect the ethos of the company. For example, dynamic, constantly changing industries assess the ability of a candidate to adjust to change and to learn new skills, whereas in steady-state industries they will test your existing skills, which can be used immediately.

The assessment centre's activities should bear some relation to the tasks required of you in the job. For example, in managerial assessment your decision-making will be tested and leadership ability.

Assessment lasts for a day or possibly two or more for senior positions and the employer will be expected to accommodate you for the duration. The location will be arranged so as to be optimally accessible for all the candidates with accessibility for candidates with disabilities.

There will usually be between five and eight candidates on a course and you should make a concerted effort to socialise and get along with these people. While you are taking part in a competitive activity you will potentially end up working with some of these people. And in any case, how you interact with your fellow candidates will be part of the assessment.

Assessment centres have always had a place in recruitment, traditionally employed for bulk recruitment campaigns at graduate or junior level. More recently there has been a trend towards applying the same techniques to more senior positions.

Some useful tips

- Ask whether the client is willing to fund transport/ hotels. Often travelling the night before and staying in a local hotel will mean you are fresher and therefore perform better on the day.

- Arrive in plenty of time on the day. There's nothing worse than running in late when the day has already begun – these assessment days run strictly to time.

- Use all coffee and lunch breaks to speak to assessors and create an impact. Ask intelligent questions and show interest in them and their business.

- Remember that you are assessed across a number of exercises. It is rare that any candidate performs well in all of the exercises so accept that some parts of the day will go better than others. Do not crumble if one exercise goes badly.

WHAT CAN AN ASSESSMENT CENTRE CONSIST OF?

Role play

- Typically based around a scenario related to the role being recruited, e.g. a fact-find and negotiation exercise for sales professionals.

- Candidates typically given a strategy paper 30 minutes prior to the role-play exercise, assessing their ability to prioritise and manage their time effectively.

- Often involves two assessors to each candidate.

- May take the form of two meetings, giving the candidate 30 minutes between the role plays to interpret and apply information gleaned from the first meeting.

- Tests a candidate's ability to perform in the role for which they have applied.

Group exercise

- Candidates are asked to work together as a group towards a stated end goal as the assessors watch and listen.
- Each individual may be given a different objective or piece of information to ensure that the exercise does not become too collegiate.
- The assessors will be looking for candidates to take control of the situation, draw opinions from the other delegates, keep the group to time, stand their ground (without becoming argumentative) and successfully take the group to its stated goal.

Behavioural event interview

- Candidates are asked to discuss two or three specific events in their career to date; for example, either key successes or events that didn't have the desired outcome.
- The assessors will then ask questions to probe around these events evaluating a candidate's approach to planning, risk analysis, decision-making, developing solutions, seeking information, developing others, customer focus, building relationships, etc.
- Individuals are typically assessed against a list of pre-agreed competencies.

Biographical interview

- Candidates are interviewed against their curriculum vitae.
- Questioning is targeted around understanding their experience/responsibilities to date, motivations, why they have made certain moves during their career, what they are looking for from their next role, key successes, qualifications, personal circumstances, current salary and expectations, etc.

- This is a more 'typical' interview that most candidates will have experienced at some point in their career to date.

Verbal and numerical testing

- Utilised to give an indication of a candidate's ability to process both verbal and numerical information while working to a time limit.
- These tests are conducted either prior to or on the assessment day and are conducted either on- or off-line.
- Candidates are often given their mark as a percentile rather than a percentage. A percentile allows your result to be compared against an appropriate control group, where 1 is the lowest and 99 is the highest.

EXAMPLES OF VERBAL CRITICAL REASONING

Verbal critical reasoning tests are used to find out how well you can assess verbal logic. They are usually in the form of a passage of prose, followed by a number of statements. Your task is to decide if the statements are 'True', 'False' or if you 'Cannot tell' from the information provided. You are to assume that everything that is said in the passages is true. Now try the example on pp 139–140.

PSYCHOMETRIC TESTS

- These are used to help assess a candidate's culture fit and psychological make-up.
- There are no right and wrong answers on these tests.
- You should answer questions honestly as opposed to trying to second-guess what the client wants to hear.

Leading scientists defend animal testing

At a recent conference sponsored by a number of leading pharmaceutical companies scientists defended the role of animal testing. The continued use of rabbits, guinea pigs, rats and mice in the development of medicines was strongly endorsed. Many delegates complained that the public did not understand that there were some products which could only be tested on live systems. Also that medical techniques such as kidney transplants would not exist were it not for pioneering animal testing. The conference confirmed that 3,000 animals had been used in tests in the previous year.

New alternative to animal testing discovered

At present there are over 10,000 ingredients available to the cosmetics industry. These can be used in the development of new products, free from the controversy surrounding animal testing. Where testing on live subjects is required this can be achieved by using groups of human volunteers, or methods which mimic the response of a particular protein Vistek which simulates the reaction of the eye. In the future, as has been the case with nuclear weapons, there is also the possibility that all testing will be modelled by computers.

Now decide if each of the statements which follow are:

True = It follows logically from the information provided
False = It is obviously incorrect given the information provided
Cannot tell = It is impossible to tell given the information provided

Statements

1. Animal testing is in decline

☐ True
☐ False
☐ Cannot tell

2. Some products can only be tested on animals

☐ True
☐ False
☐ Cannot tell

3. Animal experiments and nuclear testing make people angry

☐ True
☐ False
☐ Cannot tell

4. Vistek is a protein found in the eye

☐ True
☐ False
☐ Cannot tell

5. Animal testing has been used to develop 10,000 ingredients

☐ True
☐ False
☐ Cannot tell

Example of verbal critical reasoning test.

6. Kidney transplants were first tested in animals
- ☐ True
- ☐ False
- ☐ Cannot tell

The answers are:

1. The correct answer: Cannot tell:
   You have no idea how many animals were used in any year apart from the previous one.

2. The correct answer: True
   It says that some products can only be tested on live systems

3. The correct answer: Cannot tell
   There is no information on whether testing makes people angry.

4. The correct answer: False
   It says that Vistek simulates the reaction of the eye.

5. The correct answer: False
   It says that 10,000 ingredients can be used without the need for animal testing.

6. The correct answer: True
   It says that kidney transplants would not exist if it were not for animal testing.

Example of verbal critical reasoning test (continued)

You should not use a calculator for either of these examples.

1. A diagram on a sheet of paper is increased in size to 120% of its original size, and this copy is then reduced by 40%. What percentage of the size of the original diagram is the final copy?

   A. 28 B. 36 C. 48 D. 72 E. 80

2. What is the following approximately equal to? $5/9 + 3/4 + 5/7 =$

   A. 1 B. 2 C. 3 D. 4 E. 5

Numerical test answers: 1 = C 2 = B.

Example of a numerical test.

To have a look and take part in psychometric tests called the Keirsey Temperament Sorter II, as used in career development programmes at Fortune 500 companies and in counselling centres and career placement centres at major US universities, go to the following website: www.advisorteam.com/temperament_sorter/

Once you've registered and taken part, you will get a free temperament description and have the opportunity to buy the ten-page character report for your type.

PRESENTATION EXERCISE

- Candidates are typically asked to pre-prepare a presentation often based around a proposed business plan for/ approach to their first six months in the role that they are applying for.
- While the quality of the slides and content is important, of more importance is the delivery of the presentation and a candidate's ability to think on their feet when fielding questions.
- Candidates should run through their presentation as many times as possible, utilising their recruitment consultant either to cast a critical eye over the slides or by coming into the office to present to him/her.

17

Aspects of employment

TEMPORARY EMPLOYMENT

As a temp you are an important asset to any hiring company. It is therefore important to do what you can to ensure your success. Whatever your reason for choosing a temporary contract over permanent work, due to the nature of this type of employment you will be an important asset to any hiring company and to your agency. It is vital for all parties that your assignment as a contractor is successful as quickly as possible.

Temping CV

You may need to tailor your CV for temporary work to ensure your key skills really stand out. If you have completed a number of assignments over a long period of time, check that any gaps are accounted for. Your CV should not suggest that you haven't managed to stay anywhere for long. Ensure you can explain each role and your reason for leaving.

Interview

A temporary job may be offered with no prior meeting. Alternatively, an interview for a senior role may be as lengthy as if the role were permanent. If you are called to interview, think about your approach beforehand. You must appear committed to fulfilling your assignment, while not discounting yourself from offers of permanent work. This can be tricky. Each situation is different and direct answers are best, taking care not to concern the interviewer with too much information.

Agencies

Do some research here. Use an agency that will endeavour to match your job requirements. Try to meet your contact and ensure you understand how they operate. Return calls and emails promptly and keep the agency updated on your availability as requested.

Assignments

Once you have secured an assignment, ensure you have enough details to arrive punctually each day. Pre-check your journey and parking arrangements. Know who you should report to. Be familiar with your standard hours of work and the policy on overtime. Ensure you understand and are familiar with timesheets, paperwork required and pay arrangements. You are expected to honour your assignment for the agreed duration.

Presentation and behaviour

Ensure you are attired suitably for work, whether dress code is formal or casual. At all times be respectful of company rules. Conduct should be professional, as in a permanent job. Keep personal phone calls and emails to a minimum. Personal Internet activity is not acceptable. Do not participate in office politics.

Problems

If you are ill or unable to attend work for any reason, it is vital you inform your agency as early as possible. Failing to do this could seriously jeopardise your assignment. If there are other problems and you are unhappy with your work, again contact your agency quickly and discuss your situation with them.

EMPLOYED OR SELF-EMPLOYED?

The rules about being employed or self-employed are quite complex. If someone offers you work and gives you a 'choice' of being employed or self-employed or tells you that you are self-employed, don't assume that they know what they are talking about.

The government's local taxation department ('the Revenue') can provide all the information and guidance you require about any proposed self-employment – its terms and what agreement or contract you will need.

On the website www.hmrc.gov.uk there is a useful guide to deciding if you could be employed or self-employed. You can find it under the part of the site called 'Low Income' workers.

If you are confident that you are self-employed, the Revenue provide a lot of support for people starting up in business, and it is definitely worth visiting their site. If you do think you are self-employed, you will need to advise your local tax office within three months of your start date.

TIPS ON KEEPING YOUR JOB IN THE UK

- Be flexible – getting your foot in the door is your first step to becoming indispensable.
- Work hard – working hard and getting noticed can help ensure your job is extended (if temporary) or can lead you to promotion.
- Expect to work long hours – the UK works some of the longest hours in the world, so be prepared to adjust.
- Beat the competition – don't take no for an answer; persist with your enthusiasm to do your job and to do it well.
- Don't moan – try to stay positive.
- Don't get involved in office politics.

18

Studying in the UK

British qualifications are recognised internationally as being among the very best in the world. They can be gained at all levels from the basic to the most advanced, in a wide variety of subjects and from a wide number of institutions.

STUDENT VISA OVERVIEW

If you are a national of a country that is on the 'visa national list' (see UK visas website at www.ukvisas.gov.uk), you must obtain entry clearance known as a visa, before travelling to the UK.

If you are a national of the USA, Canada, South Africa, Singapore, Malaysia, South Korea, Hong Kong (unless you are a British National Overseas), Japan, Australia or New Zealand and you are coming to the UK for more than six months, you must obtain entry clearance from your nearest British diplomatic post (Embassy or High Commission) before travelling to the UK. If you arrive without entry clearance you will not be allowed to enter the UK.

If your country is not on either of the lists (the UK visas list or the country list above), and entry clearance is not compulsory for you, it is recommended that you get optional entry clearance (known as an 'entry certificate' rather than a visa) in the following circumstances:

- if you are coming to the UK as a student with your family
- if you are coming to the UK as a 'prospective student'
- if you are coming to the UK to do a course of six months or less.

You should apply for entry clearance, either in the form of a visa or an entry certificate, before you come to the UK by contacting the British Embassy or High Commission in your country.

CONDITIONS OF BEING A STUDENT IN THE UK

The UK immigration requires students who wish to study in the UK to meet certain conditions that relate to:

- the place where they wish to study
- the course selected
- ability of the person to follow the course
- finances of the person applying
- intentions during and after the study programme is finished.

The British government's UK visas website has full details of visa conditions and should be checked regularly in case there are any changes to the general information supplied above. Further details about visas are shown in Chapter 9.

FINDING A UK-BASED COURSE

What information should I check about the institution I want to study at?

Since 1 January 2005, UK immigration permission (visas, entry clearance and leave to remain) is now granted only for study at institutions which are listed in the Register of Education and Training Providers, compiled by the UK Government Department for Education and Skills (DfES).

It is very important that you check whether the institution you want to attend is in the Register before you make your immigration application. If the institution is not in the Register, your application will be refused and you might have no right of appeal.

The following education and training providers are automatically included in the Register:

- those that receive public funding
- institutions that are accredited through the British Council, the British Accreditation Council, or the Association of British Language Schools
- institutions that have been inspected and approved by government inspection bodies.

All other institutions have to apply to be added to the Register. However, their inclusion provides no guarantee of the quality or standards of their provision.

For more information about the Register of Providers, please see the DfES website at www.dfes.gov.uk/providersregister.

The Internet is a great place to find out what courses are available for studying in the UK. The British Council website in particular is a good source of information; see www.educationuk.org.

www.Hotcourses.com and UCAS www.ucas.com can also help you search and apply for courses in the UK. Many individual institutions such as Fulham and Chelsea College also carry details of their own specific UK courses on their own website; see www.fccollege.co.uk.

Once you find a course that interests you, email, telephone or write to the institution and ask them to send you their prospectus. This is a booklet which provides information on all the courses they run and the facilities they offer. All prospectuses should be free of charge. The British Council's offices outside the UK hold copies of prospectuses from many UK institutions. To find your nearest British Council office, go to www.educationuk.org.

DEGREE COURSES

There is an official list of institutions that offer recognised UK degrees on the UK government's Department of Education and Skill's website www.dfes.gov.uk/recognisedukdegrees/. Degree courses can be taken at universities, higher education colleges, colleges of further education and colleges of art. Degrees are awarded at two levels – undergraduate or first degree and postgraduate or higher degree. The most prestigious universities in the UK to obtain a degree are Oxford or Cambridge. However, you will need excellent marks or a scholarship to study there.

Applications to universities for undergraduate degree level courses must be made through a central admissions system called Universities and Colleges Admissions System (UCAS). The UCAS website www.ucas.com contains a great deal of information specifically for international students and offers an online application facility.

VOCATIONAL AND FURTHER EDUCATION

These courses are very popular in the UK and are designed to prepare you for a particular career, give you access to higher education or give you increased skill for a career you are already pursuing. UK qualifications you can attain include National

Vocational Qualifications (NVQs) and Scottish Vocational Qualification (SVQs), Business and Technology Education Council (BTEC) Diplomas and Certificates, City and Guilds awards and Royal Society of Arts (RSA) qualifications.

PROFESSIONAL QUALIFICATIONS

Some professions in the UK require you to take professional qualifications in order for you to practise, e.g. law, medicine and architecture. Many professions in engineering, finance and nursing also have their own professional institutions, e.g. the Institute of Bankers; Chartered Institute of Marketing; Institute of Civil Engineers.

Professional bodies award their own qualifications based on examinations, but rarely will they run their own courses. Courses for such professional qualifications are instead run by colleges and universities, so you'll need to contact your professional body for details about who offers their courses, or search the main search engines, such as Google, Yahoo!, etc., to find out the information for yourself.

POSTGRADUATE COURSES

If you want to study in London at one of the better private colleges for international students, give Fulham and Chelsea College a look. It is centrally located and offers a range of professional business diploma courses that include travel, tourism and hospitality. The courses run for one year but you can start them at any time, as they offer a blended learning system. So whenever you want to come to the UK to study you can start one of their courses. Visit www.fccollege.co.uk for more details.

Lots of other postgraduate courses are offered throughout the UK. To see a full range of courses visit the British Council website, www.britishcouncil.org.

SHORT COURSES AND PART-TIME STUDY

Many part-time courses are run throughout the week and/or during the evenings and weekends. Visit www.floodlight.co.uk for just some of the ones currently available.

FINDING SCHOLARSHIPS

You should contact your local British Council office about any scholarships that are currently available to students from your country who wish to study in the UK. The British Council has representatives in 110 countries across the world and their website provides all the details you need about current scholarships, eligibility, how to apply and how you can obtain application forms (most of which are downloadable from the site).

Scholarships administered by the British Council tend to be allocated more than one academic year in advance so you should start enquiring at least 18 months in advance of your proposed start date.

For your nearest British Council office outside the UK and for more information on scholarships and studying in the UK, visit www.britishcouncil.org/.

STUDY METHODS IN THE UK

Although exact methods do vary according to the subject you are studying and the institution you are studying at, the structure of most courses fall into either timetabled classes, or a few hours timetabled and the majority of your time working independently. So what learning methods can you expect from a UK course? The following is a general guide from UKCOSA www.ukcosa.org.uk, the UK's Council for International Education.

Lectures

These are large classes, usually lasting around one hour, where a lecturer (or tutor) talks about a subject and the students take notes. On some courses there can be over 100 students in a lecture. There is usually little or no opportunity to ask questions during the lecture. Lectures are usually intended to:

- guide you through the course material by explaining the main points of a topic
- introduce new topics for further study or debate
- give the most up-to-date information that may not be included in textbooks.

Seminars

These are smaller classes where students and a tutor discuss a topic. Seminars often last longer than lectures. You will know in advance what the topic is, and the tutor will usually ask some students to prepare a short presentation for discussion. Seminars are usually intended to encourage debate about an issue. This means different opinions will be expressed by the tutor and students. The aim is not for students to be told the 'correct' answer, but to understand the different arguments and make judgements about their merits. This process helps you learn to analyse a topic critically.

Tutorials

These are meetings between a tutor and an individual student or small group of students. Tutorials are usually intended to give you more focused guidance on:

- a piece of work you are doing
- a piece of work you have already completed
- a problem you may be having with a topic or with study methods.

Practical work

On many courses you will have practical workshops, e.g. laboratories on science courses, performance classes in music or drama, a mock trial on a law course. On some courses (e.g. geography) you may go on field trips away from the institution. You may work individually but more usually you will be part of a group. Practical classes are usually intended to give you practical experience of the theories you learn in other classes and to develop practical skills.

Workplace training

On some courses you will have training in a working environment, under the supervision of experienced staff (e.g. working in a hospital on a nursing or medicine course). Other courses offer 'sandwich' placements – an opportunity to spend time away from classes working in employment related to your course of study.

Independent study

On any course you will be expected to do some independent study. This usually involves working on your own (or sometimes in a small group with other students) to research a topic and produce written work, or make a presentation at a seminar. This is an integral part of UK academic culture. Independent study is intended to:

- help you develop skills such as critical analysis and problem-solving
- develop your research skills (e.g. finding relevant books and articles)
- allow you to investigate a topic in more detail and develop your own ideas.

Written work

You will almost certainly be asked to produce written work, usually through independent study. Written work may include:

- essays
- a project or a dissertation (a long essay based on extensive independent research, data collection or experimentation)
- assignment questions (e.g. a series of mathematical problems).

Written work is often assessed. This may be to monitor your progress and identify areas for improvement or it may contribute to your overall mark or grade for the course.

Other projects and assignments

On some courses you may also be asked to produce work in other forms. For example, you may be asked to write a computer program, prepare a poster presentation about a topic, or prepare practical work for evaluation.

Group work

You may be asked to undertake a piece of work jointly with other students, which may either lead to joint or separate assessment.

Group work is designed to encourage team-working skills. If your group includes students from different countries, you may find you have different views and expectations about how work will be shared and decisions made. Group work can be a good way of learning about working in a multicultural environment.

Examinations and assessments

UK institutions use many different forms of assessment, including:

- 'closed' examinations, where you are not allowed to refer to books or notes and have a specific time to complete a certain number of questions
- 'open' examinations, where you can refer to books and notes and may even be able to take the question paper away and return it by a certain time
- assessed essays, individual projects and dissertations
- group work projects
- portfolios (a collection of work)
- presentations to a seminar
- a display or performance of work (e.g. an art show or music performance)
- practical assessments (e.g. in laboratories or on hospital wards).

Some courses are continuously assessed, meaning that instead of examinations at the end of the year, your progress is assessed and marked throughout the year.

Plagiarism

Plagiarism means presenting someone else's work as your own. If you present the words or ideas of an author or another student without acknowledging the source, you could be accused of plagiarism.

Whenever you use a quotation from a book, or reproduce an author's ideas (even in your own words), you should indicate the source. This process is known as referencing. You may find the accepted ways of quoting and referencing work in the UK are different from those you are used to. Penalties for plagiarism, especially in assessed work and examinations, can be very severe, and may include failing the course. Most academic departments have a preferred style of referencing. *Check with your tutor about how you should reference your work: don't rely on the advice of other students/friends.*

Seeking help

Lecturers and tutors will normally be available to provide help and advice on a very limited basis outside timetabled classes. You should try to ask your questions during tutorials or you may be able to see staff during their 'office hour', a designated time during the week when they are available to see students.

Lecture notes

When you attend lectures, you will need to take notes. Remember:

- you don't need to write down everything the lecturer says: concentrate on the main points and important details
- most lecturers use asides (stories to illustrate a point), examples and even jokes – you don't need to write all of these down
- abbreviations and symbols for common words and terms can help you write faster, but use ones that you will understand later
- if there is something you don't understand, make a note to ask after the lecture or in a tutorial

- keep your notes in order in a file; most students write up their notes neatly after a lecture
- don't just file the notes away until your exams; read through them regularly: this will help with revision
- if you want to record a lecture on tape, ask the lecturer's permission first.

Don't worry if you find it difficult to understand the lecturer. This will get easier as you get used to their style and, if you are not a native speaker, as your English improves.

Seminar contributions

Seminars can be intimidating if you are not used to this kind of teaching. Don't worry. Many other students feel the same at first. Participating actively in seminars is an important part of the learning process, so try to contribute, even if it seems difficult at first. It is best to do some reading before each seminar, so that you are familiar with the topic and can follow and contribute to the discussion. It may help you to make notes before the seminar of any points you would like to make. If you are having difficulty in seminars, discuss this with your tutor.

Reading

On most courses you will be given a book list. You will not usually be expected to buy or even read every book and journal article on the list. Items on a book list may contain:

- essential, basic reading or reference material for the course
- an overview of the subject
- background information

- useful information for a specific topic or piece of work.

Check with your tutor and other students who are already studying the course which books are essential for you to buy. Most books will be available in your institution's library but essential titles ('core' texts) may be difficult to borrow because everyone on the course needs them. You may be able to reduce the cost of buying books by:

- buying second-hand editions (from students in later stages of the course, or from a second-hand bookshop) – but make sure you buy an up-to-date version
- forming a group with other students on the course, each buying some of the books and sharing them.

UK ACADEMIC CULTURE

It may take some time for you to adjust to studying in the UK. Academic culture and expectations vary according to the subject, the level of study and the type of institution. However, there are some general trends that you may notice in the UK:

- students often work independently, studying on their own for significant periods of time
- students are expected to develop critical judgment, which means an ability to assess whether an argument is coherent and well supported by evidence
- learning large amounts of factual data is important in some subject areas, but in many cases a critical approach is considered more important.

Many UK students will also be going through the process of learning the conventions of academic life. Study skills classes may help you understand what is required. Your tutors should also be able to guide you as to how to approach your work.

KNOW WHAT IS REQUIRED

It is important to know what you need to do to fulfil the course requirements. By finding out the answers to some of the following questions, you may be able to plan your work and how to use your time effectively:

- When writing an essay or assignment, how long should it be?
- Is a piece of work assessed, or is it for 'practice'?
- What proportion of your marks does a piece of work or examination represent?
- How much work will you have to do, and at what stage in the course?

Much of this information may be included in a course handbook: this will be a useful reference throughout the course.

SOURCES OF ADVICE AND HELP

If you have a question or problem with your studies, ask your tutors; they will usually be happy to advise you, or put you in touch with other sources of help. It is best to seek advice early, rather than wait for a problem to become critical.

FEES FOR UK COURSES

Tuition fees and living costs can soon add up. You need to consider the total cost of your course in the UK including the length of time you will be in the country, the typical amount you need to live on, travel expenses, books, equipment and socialising costs.

Fees can vary and aren't necessarily an indication of the quality of the course. Degree courses range from £5,000 to £10,000 per year. Generally, science courses are more expensive than arts or business courses. All institutions publish course fees on their websites or include them in their prospectuses.

ENTRANCE QUALIFICATIONS FOR STUDY IN THE UK

Many countries have their own education and qualification systems. You can check the equivalence of your country's qualifications with those in the UK by contacting the National Academic Information Centre (NARIC) www.naric.org.uk. Alternatively, the international recruitment staff at the institution where you wish to study may also be able to advise you.

Career-based courses depend on relevant skills or experience. Degree courses require at least three A-levels or equivalent. For entry to taught postgraduate courses you will need an undergraduate degree or equivalent from your country in a relevant area. For a doctorate programme (PhD) you will need a UK master's degree or equivalent from your country.

ATTENDING UK INTERVIEWS TO FINALISE YOUR PLACE ON A COURSE

It is very important that you request permission ('leave') to enter the

UK as a prospective student rather than as a visitor in order to attend interviews to finalise your study place on a course. You will be expected to provide evidence that you have made contact with UK institutions, e.g. letters inviting you for interview in the UK. Prospective students can stay in the UK for up to six months to make arrangements for their studies. Once you have enrolled at an institution, you will need to extend your stay in the UK as a student. If you have not come to the UK in the immigration category of 'prospective student', you may not be able to do this in the UK and may have to return to your country to make this application.

STUDYING FOR SIX MONTHS OR MORE

If you apply to come to the UK as a student to complete a course of six months or more, you will be given a passport stamp or visa sticker that allows you to work part-time during the term (up to 20 hours per week) and full-time during the vacations. However, for immigration purposes students must be able to show that they can afford to study and live in the UK without having to work. Further details regarding visa categories and the legal requirements for entry are shown in Chapter 9.

After you have completed your studies it may be possible for you to stay in the UK for practical training, work experience or full-time employment. The UK government has a scheme called 'Training and Work Experience Scheme' where employers can apply for permits to employ a person in a particular post for a limited period for work experience or professional training.

The government has also relaxed its policy on students staying on in the UK after studies under the main 'Work Permit' scheme. Degree-level students, student nurses and postgraduate doctors and dentists in training may be able to stay in the UK for work permit employment if their employer can secure a work permit for them.

It may also be possible to stay on in the UK under the 'Innovators Scheme' and the 'Highly Skilled Migrant Programme' for those who are classed as highly experienced and/or highly qualified students.

Other government schemes have also been introduced, such as the Science and Engineering Graduates Scheme (introduced in October 2004) and the Fresh Talent Scotland Scheme (launched in summer 2005) which may also enable students to remain in the UK to work for a limited period after they successfully complete their studies.

Regulations and categories for visas to the UK, including the schemes mentioned above, are covered in detail in Chapters 3–16.

WORK VISAS

You must ensure you have the correct visa to work in the UK. Failure to have a valid working visa or to comply with its conditions may result in deportation. For further detailed information on Visas see Chapters 3–11.

BRINGING A DEPENDANT TO THE UK WHILE YOU STUDY

If you are studying for 12 months or more then your husband/wife/son/daughter arriving in the UK with you should be given a passport stamp which allows him or her to work. Only your spouse and your children are permitted to come with you to the UK while you study, but your children must be under the ages of 18 years when they first enter the UK. Further information about dependants of international students can be found at www.ukcosa.org.uk.

SCHOOLING FOR YOUR CHILDREN WHILE YOU STUDY

If you have brought your children with you, and they are aged between 5 and 16 years old, they can attend state primary and secondary schools in the UK, as long as they are here as your dependants. You will not have to pay for this. However, some schools may sometimes refuse places to children if they consider their stay in the UK will be too short, or if they have no more places. Further information about dependants of international students can be found at www.ukcosa.org.uk.

NEW RULES ABOUT STUDENT SUPPORT FOR EU NATIONALS (16 AUGUST 05, FIRST POSTED 6 JUNE 05)

Following the case of *Bidar* in the European Court of Justice, the law has been changed in all nations of the UK with regard to student support for EU nationals. The following additional categories of student are now eligible for student support and, in Scotland, for 'home' fees.

Scotland

In Scotland, you will be eligible for 'home' fees and student support, and liable for the graduate endowment, if:

- you are a national of a member state of the European Union other than the United Kingdom, or the child of such a national
- you are ordinarily resident in Scotland on the relevant date (at the start of the course)
- you have been ordinarily resident in the UK and Islands throughout the three-year period before that date.

Northern Ireland

In Northern Ireland, EU nationals and their children, including UK nationals, are eligible for full student support. You must be ordinarily resident in Northern Ireland on the first day of the first academic year of your course and you must have been ordinarily resident in the UK and Islands for the three-year period before that date. This new category does not apply to fees assessments.

Wales and England

In Wales and England, you will be eligible for full student support if:

- you are an EU national (the children of EU nationals are not included); and
- you are ordinarily resident in England or Wales on the first day of the first academic year of the course
- you have been ordinarily resident in the UK and Islands for the three-year period before the first day of the first academic year of the course.

In addition:

- if you are a UK national you must have a right to be treated no less favourably than a national of another member state because you have exercised a Community right of free movement, e.g. you must have worked or studied in one or more countries in the European Economic Area, other than the UK
- if you are of any EU nationality and your only or main reason for being in the UK and Islands was to receive full-time education, you must have been ordinarily resident in the European

Economic Area immediately before your three-year period of ordinary residence in the UK and Islands.

For more information about 'home' fees and student support, see the UKCOSA website www.ukcosa.org.uk.

New rights for same-sex partners

From 5 December 2005, same-sex couples in the UK will be able to register a civil partnership and acquire very similar rights and responsibilities to those who are in opposite-sex marriages. This applies to international students who want to enter into a civil partnership in the UK. It also means that international students who have formalised an equivalent legal relationship in another country may be able to bring their same-sex partner to the UK as their dependant, in the same way that students can currently be accompanied by their husband or wife.

For more information about how these new rights will apply in relation to UK immigration law, see the website of the Immigration and Nationality Directorate of the Home Office, www.ind.homeoffice.gov.uk/ind/en/home/applying/general_caseworking/civil_partnership.html.

For general information about civil partnerships and for details of partnerships in other countries that are regarded as equivalent to UK civil partnerships, see the website of the Women and Equality Unit of the Department of Trade and Industry at www.womenandequalityunit.gov.uk/lgbt/faq.htm.

HEALTHCARE FOR YOU AND YOUR FAMILY WHILE YOU STUDY

If you course lasts for six months or more, you can receive treatment from the National Health Service (NHS) from the beginning of your stay. You will not have to pay for hospital treatment but you may have to pay for some dental treatment and a standard charge (called a prescription charge) for medicines prescribed by a doctor, although in some cases these charges are waived. The NHS treatment available is also available to your husband or wife and children. As a general rule, children under 16 years old or under 19 years old and in full-time education, do not normally have to pay for any NHS treatments. To keep up to date with the latest news go to www.ukcosa.org.uk.

FINDING A JOB WHILE YOU STUDY

There is plenty of help and advice in the preceding chapters on finding general employment, creating a CV, interview techniques and much more. Lots of students also use the site www.gumtree.com to look for jobs, among other things.

STUDENT DISCOUNT CARD

Being a student entitles you to various discounts for shopping, travel, movies and lots more. When you enrol to study in the UK you will be given an International Student Card (ISIC) application form. Once you complete the form you will need to attach a passport photograph, have a copy of your enrolment letter from your college and pay a small fee in the form of a cheque (if you have a bank account) or a postal order, which you can obtain from any UK post office. The form is then posted to the ISIC and within about two weeks you should receive your card. For more information about the card visit: www.isiccard.com.

LONDON TRANSPORT STUDENT TRAVEL DISCOUNT CARD

If you are based in London, a London Transport student card entitles you to 30 per cent off your travel in London – which includes the underground and the bus network. These forms are also available from the college you've chosen to study at and should be completed in the same way as the ISIC application. You normally receive your card by post within two weeks and then you must show your card whenever you purchase your London travel cards in order to obtain a discount.

OTHER USEFUL STUDENT INFORMATION SITES

www.skill.org.uk Skill: National Bureau for Students with Disabilities. Skill operates an information and advice service and works with members and volunteers to promote equality of opportunity for students with disabilities.

www.naric.org.uk UK NARIC: the National Academic Recognition and Information Centre. NARIC advises on the recognition of non-UK qualifications.

www.hero.ac.uk HERO: Higher Education and Research Opportunities in the UK. HERO is the official gateway site to the UK's universities, colleges and research organisations

www.cisuk.org.uk/ Council for International Students. An organisation of and for international students in the UK.

19

Basic employment laws

The information in this section has been taken from the Trades Union Congress (TUC) websites www.tuc.org.uk and www.worksmart.org.uk. It is reproduced with the kind permission of the TUC and is subject to copyright. © Trades Union Congress 2006. The TUC is the national centre for British trade unions.

Although the advice given in this chapter is as accurate as the publishers can ensure, nothing in this text constitutes legal advice, which should always be sought from a legal practitioner.

YOUR JOB AND THE LAW

Everyone at work has basic legal rights, and there are new ones on the way thanks both to Europe and new laws from the UK government. Employment law can be complex and you should always take further advice. Your own rights will depend on your own circumstances so you should always take detailed legal advice on your situation.

YOUR CONTRACT OF EMPLOYMENT

Most employers will give you a written contract of employment as soon as you have accepted a job or on your first day of a new job.

Sometimes you may be given a contract of employment without realising it. It could be contained in your letter of appointment. It might be called something different, such as a staff handbook. It is not unusual to find a note at the front of a staff handbook saying which sections are part of the legal contract of employment and which bits simply supply useful information.

ARE YOU AN EMPLOYEE OR A WORKER?

Even if your employer does not give you a written contract, some kind of basic contract exists in law as soon as you are paid. But although many people think this is a contract of employment, it may not be so.

This is because you can work for somebody or an organisation in two ways. Most people are employees, and should have a contract of employment. It may be for a fixed term, but as an employee you get the legal rights set out below.

The alternative is a 'contract for services'. This is where you are paid to carry out a particular task in return for a fee of some kind. In this situation you are self-employed and do not have rights as an employee. Confusingly the Inland Revenue uses a different definition of 'self-employed', so you should always be very clear about your position.

TWO KINDS OF EMPLOYMENT RIGHT

You have two kinds of rights at work. The first are those given to you by the law called statutory rights. The second are those provided by your contract of employment. They will be different for every job. Normally they will be better than the legal minimum or cover areas where there are no statutory rights. These are called contractual rights. (The only case where a contract of employment can reduce your statutory rights is that employees on fixed term contracts of more than two years can sign away their right to statutory redundancy pay.)

Both types of employment rights can be enforced in law. Usually this is carried out at an Employment Tribunal. If you think your employer is acting against your contractual rights, take further advice.

YOUR RIGHTS TIMETABLE

Not all employment rights start from your first day at work. Your contract of employment may set out how you get extra or better rights once you have been in your job for a period of time. For example, holiday rights often increase with length of service. The same is true of your statutory rights.

When you apply for a job, you should not be discriminated against in a job selection process because of your sex, race, disability or because you are a trade union member.

From your first day at work, you should be given a statement showing how much you earn and any deductions that will be made from your pay. (This is not the same as a contract of employment, although a contract of employment can contain this information.) Your rights include the following:

- Time off for maternity leave even if you were pregnant when you started the job.
- Emergency leave.
- Time off for antenatal care.
- Protection from dismissal on some limited grounds including pregnancy, whistle-blowing and trade union activity.
- Working time rights.
- You have the right not to be discriminated against for reasons of your sex, including being pregnant, your race or any disability, or for being a member of a trade union.

- You have a right to equal pay with members of the opposite sex doing the same or a comparable job to you.
- A minimum wage. More information on the minimum wage can be obtained from the government's minimum wage helpline, 0845 845 0360.
- You are entitled to work in a place which is safe and does not cause you to injure yourself or become ill.
- You have a right to time off to study if you are 16 or 17 years old.
- You have a right not to have deductions made from your pay unless you have agreed to them.
- You have a right to time off for public or trade union duties.
- You can claim breach of contract if your employer sacks you without giving you the agreed notice, or breaks some other term in your contract of employment.
- If you are paying National Insurance contributions, you can claim Statutory Sick Pay after you have been off sick for four days in a row.
- You have a right to be accompanied by your trade union or a workplace colleague in a disciplinary or grievance procedure.

After a month, you have the right to:

- one week's notice of dismissal
- payment if you are suspended on medical grounds
- wages if you are laid off.

After two months, you have the right to a written statement of your terms of employment which must include your pay, hours, where you are expected to work, holidays and other benefits such as pension entitlement. While the written statement is not a contract of employment, it is very important that you have one as it can be used if necessary in a court or tribunal if problems do arise.

After one year, you are entitled to claim unfair dismissal if your employer sacks you without good reason, or without allowing you to go through a proper dismissal procedure at work. You are also entitled to written reasons for dismissal from your employer. You cannot be made to 'waive' your right to claim unfair dismissal, even if you are on a short-term contract.

You can take up to 13 weeks unpaid parental leave to care for a child during its first five years. Rights also apply to adopted children and are increased if your child is disabled.

After two years, you can claim statutory redundancy pay if your job has ended and no-one has been taken on to do it. The amount depends on your age, your pay and your length of service. You may get more if your contract provides for it.

Holidays

Most working people aged 16 and over are entitled to at least four weeks' paid holiday per year. Holidays from work need to be booked in advance and with your employer's agreement.

YOUR WORKING TIME RIGHTS

People in Britain work longer hours than anywhere else in Europe. However, Europe's working time directive covers most workers and entitles them to:

- four weeks' paid holiday a year
- a break when the working day is more than six hours
- a rest period of 11 hours every working day
- a rest period of 24 hours once every seven days
- a ceiling of 48 hours on the maximum average working week

- a ceiling of an average of eight hours' night work in every 24
- free health assessment for night workers.

The working time directive is complex so for more information visit the Department of Trade and Industry's website at http://www.dti.gov.uk/er/index.htm.

FAMILY FRIENDLY? RIGHTS FOR PARENTS

New rights for all new parents and better maternity rights are beginning to help make work more family-friendly. These include the following:

- Maternity leave and maternity pay.
- Paternity leave and pay.
- Adoption leave and pay.
- Parental leave – for every child including adopted children, mums and dads are entitled to take up to 13 weeks' unpaid parental leave before the child's fifth birthday (or the fifth anniversary of the adoption). But it must be taken in blocks of at least a week, and no more than four weeks can be taken in any one year. You must give 21 days' notice, and an employer can make you postpone it for up to six months except when you are asking for leave when your child is born or adopted. Many employers will probably be more flexible about some of these conditions. Parents of disabled children can take single days off and leave can be taken up to the child's 18th birthday.
- Emergency family leave – you are now entitled to unpaid leave for family emergencies when you have to care for a child or other dependant such as an elderly parent in an emergency.

YOUR DISMISSAL RIGHTS

If you have just lost your job, your rights will depend on how long you have worked for your current employer and why you have been sacked. Losing your job is about the worst possible thing that can happen to you at work and you should take further advice from your union or other advice agency.

There are three basic ways you can lose your job:

- through redundancy (this is when your job is no longer required)
- you have been dismissed fairly – this will be either because of serious misconduct by you, because you cannot do your job properly or because you do not enjoy legal protection from unfair dismissal
- you have been unfairly dismissed and can take your employer to a tribunal.

What can a tribunal do?

A tribunal can order an employer to give you your job back. However, this is fairly unusual. Usually the tribunal will order your former employer to pay you compensation. The average award is around £3,000.

Treated unfairly?

The law protects everyone at work from being discriminated against because of their race, their sex or a disability. This protection covers pay and conditions, promotion and all treatment at work, including the job interview.

There is no legal protection against discrimination on other grounds such as age or because you are gay or lesbian. But if you are sacked on these grounds, and you have worked for the same employer for more than a year you might be able to claim unfair dismissal.

For further advice here are some useful contacts:

Citizens Advice Bureau www.citizensadvice.org.uk/
Equal Opportunities Commission www.eoc.org.uk/ for sex discrimination
Commission for Racial Equality www.cre.gov.uk/
Disability Gov UK www.direct.gov.uk/DisabledPeople
LAGER (Lesbian and Gay Employment Rights) 020 7704 8066 (lesbians) and 020 7704 6066 (gay men).

HEALTH AND SAFETY

You and your employer have rights and responsibilities under health and safety law.

- Your employer has a duty to make sure you are not injured or made ill at work.
- You have a duty to work safely by co-operating with your employer, and following safety guidelines.
- Your employer has a duty to train you to deal with health and safety issues.
- All workplaces must have an accident book in which work-related injuries must be recorded.
- Your employer must inform and consult you or your union representative on all health and safety issues.

- You have a right to refuse to do something dangerous if you feel you are in 'imminent and serious danger'.

There are many special regulations about the handling of dangerous substances or processes and the use of machinery. These normally have to be displayed or made available to staff. Read them carefully.

The Health and Safety Executive (HSE) enforce and advise on the law. For more information visit www.hse.gov.uk or call 0845 345 005.

TAKING A CASE TO AN EMPLOYMENT TRIBUNAL

Employment tribunals are a special kind of court that deal with employment issues. They are more informal than courts of law. Sometimes lawyers are involved, but in more straightforward cases people will use a union officer or someone from an advice agency, or present their own cases.

Costs cannot normally be recovered in employment tribunal cases, so if you employ a lawyer you will have to pay their fee out of any damages or compensation you win.

Complaints must be made within three calendar months of the event happening. This is extended to six months for redundancy and equal-pay issues. To make a case to an employment tribunal you need to fill in a form called an ET1. You can get this from your union, your local job centre or Unemployment Benefit Office. Most cases in employment tribunals are about unfair dismissal, but other examples have included:

- unauthorised deduction from wages
- sex, race and disability discrimination
- equal pay
- failure to receive the national minimum wage.

TRADE UNIONS

Trade unions are organisations that represent people at work. Their purpose is to protect and improve people's pay and conditions of employment. They also campaign for laws and policies which will benefit working people.

Trade unions exist because an individual worker has very little power to influence decisions that are made about his or her job. By joining together with other workers, there is more chance of having a voice and influence.

The Trades Union Congress (TUC) is the national centre for British trade unions. Individual trade unions affiliate to the TUC by paying a yearly fee. The TUC has 65 UK unions in membership, representing nearly 6.5 million working people from all walks of life. The TUC campaigns for a fair deal at work and for social justice at home and abroad.

To find out if an employer recognises a union and/or to find out which union is best to join in order to represent your profession, visit the TUC's website at www.worksmart.org.uk and www.tuc.org.uk and follow the links for 'Unions'.

MORE ADVICE

ACAS is a public body that promotes good workplace relations. Contact them on 08457 47 47 47 or visit www.acas.org.uk.

The TUC operate a 'Know Your Rights Telephone Line' on 0870 600 4882 (national rate, 8am–10pm) where you can order information booklets on your employment rights and other workplace issues. They also operate workSMART, where a range of free guides are available helping working people get the best from work; see www.worksmart.org.uk. Or visit their main website at www.tuc.org.uk, which is a one-stop shop for the very latest information on workers' rights and their latest campaigns.

20

National Insurance and taxation

OBTAINING A NATIONAL INSURANCE NUMBER

If you work in the UK you will need to obtain a National Insurance (NI) number. National Insurance will be deducted from your pay by your employer. It is a form of taxation used by the government to pays for pensions, state benefits (sickness pay, disability allowance, unemployment benefit, etc.) and is used to fund the UK's free National Health Service (NHS), which is one of the best in Europe.

NI numbers are issued by the Department for Work and Pensions (DWP). You will need to call them, give them your postcode and work details and they will let you know the location of your local office. You will then need to call your local office (sometimes this will be at your local job centre) and make an appointment to receive your NI number. When you go for your interview you will generally need to take your passport, a letter from your employer or letters showing you are registered with employment agencies looking for work, and two or three other forms of ID. Generally, it takes six to eight weeks after your interview for your NI number to be sent to your UK address in the post.

Useful contacts

www.dwp.gov.uk/ Department for work and pensions
www.jobcentreplus.gov.uk Job centres

The rates of NI you pay vary so check out the rate that may apply to you on http://www.hmrc.gov.uk/.

For information about what, how and who can receive the free services from the NHS, please see www.nhs.uk/ and www.nhsdirect.nhs.uk.

TAXATION

As in most countries, the UK requires you to pay tax on your earnings. In the UK there is a staggered taxation system based on the more you earn the more you pay. The highest rate of tax is 40 per cent on amounts in excess of £32,400 per annum.

Rates and allowances – income tax

Income tax allowances	**2005–06 (£)**	**2006–07 (£)**
Personal allowance	4,895	5,035
Personal allowance for people aged 65–74	7,090	7,280
Personal allowance for people aged 75 and over	7,220	7,420
Income limit for age-related allowances	19,500	20,100
Married couple's allowance for people born before 6 April 1935	5,905	6,065
Married couple's allowance – aged 75 or more	5,975	6,135
Minimum amount of married couple's allowance	2,280	2,350
Blind person's allowance	1,610	1,660

The rate of relief for the continuing married couple's allowance and maintenance relief for people born before 6 April 1935, and for the children's tax credit, is 10 per cent.

Taxable Bands

Taxable Bands Allowances	**2005–06 (£)**	**2006–07 (£)**
Starting rate 10%	0 – 2,090	0 – 2,150
Basic rate 22%	2,091 – 32,400	2,151 – 33,300
Higher rate 40%	Over 32,400	over 33,300

The tax year runs from 6 April until 5 April the following year and HM Revenue and Customs (HMRC) is the department responsible for the business of the former Inland Revenue and HM Customs and Excise www.hmrc.gov.uk/.

The first time you start working in the UK your employer will complete and submit a P46 form to HMRC. Until you receive your tax code from the Revenue you will be taxed at the basic rate of tax, which is 22 per cent. Once you are issued with a code, your tax will be adjusted. If your tax code is not adjusted by the end of the year you will have to apply to the Revenue to reclaim any tax you consider you've overpaid. Alternatively, if you haven't paid enough tax you will be liable to pay any additional amount of tax due based on your total earnings for the year.

TAXATION FOR COMPANY OWNERS

If you are a limited company, the tax liability decreases and you pay corporation tax of 19 per cent on your gross earnings, rather than the standard basic personal rate of tax of 22 per cent.

As long as your earnings (salaries and dividends) don't exceed £32,400 in a tax year, you do not have to pay any additional personal tax.

Running your own limited company in the UK is subject to many regulations, so always consult the relevant professionals to ensure you have the most up-to-date information and are complying with the appropriate laws. The most useful site for limited company information is: www.companieshouse.gov.uk/, or call their helpline on 0870 3333636.

21

Starting a business

This chapter is based on information on the Companies House website: www.companieshouses.gov.uk.

UK LAW

UK legislation changes all the time. Since the late 1980s copy of all UK legislation has been available online from HMSO, where you can also order your own printed copy if you require. Visit www.opsi.gov.uk/legislation/uk.htm.

FORMING YOUR OWN COMPANY

For further information regarding the type of visas and the regulations around being able to form your own company in the UK, see Chapters 3–11. Other useful contacts include: www.businesslink.gov.uk and www.companieshouse.gov.uk/.

New companies

There are four main types of UK company:

- Private company limited by shares – members' liability is limited to the amount unpaid on shares they hold. This includes those community interest companies (CICs) which are private companies limited by shares.
- Private company limited by guarantee – members' liability is limited to the amount they have agreed to contribute to the company's assets if it is wound up. This includes all RTM (Right to Manage) companies, commonhold associations and those

community interest companies which are companies limited by guarantee.

- Private unlimited company – there is no limit to the members' liability.

- Public limited company (PLC) – the company's shares may be offered for sale to the general public and members' liability is limited to the amount unpaid on shares held by them. This also includes community interest public limited companies (that is, CICs which are PLCs).

Company incorporation

The Companies Act generally allows one or more persons to form a company for any lawful purpose by subscribing to its memorandum of association. However, a public company or an unlimited company must have at least two subscribers.

Ready-made companies are available from company formation agents, whose names and addresses appear in the media or on Internet search engines. If you incorporate a company yourself, you will be responsible for filing a range of documents at Companies House, including the following.

Memorandum of association

This document sets out:

- the company's name

- where the registered office of the company is situated (in England, Wales or Scotland)

- what it will do (its objects). The object of a company may simply be to carry on business as a general commercial company
- other clauses to be included in the memorandum depend on the type of company being incorporated.

The company's memorandum delivered to the Registrar must be signed by each subscriber in front of a witness who must attest the signature.

Articles of association

This document sets out the rules for the running of the company's internal affairs. All companies that are limited by guarantee or unlimited, and all community interest companies (whether limited by shares or by guarantee) must register articles.

In addition, the articles for community interest companies must comply with the requirements of the Community Interest Company Regulations 2005. Sample CIC memoranda and articles can be found on the CIC website, www.cicregulator.gov.uk.

The company's articles delivered to the Registrar must be signed by each subscriber in front of a witness, who must attest the signature.

What is a registered office?

It is the address of a company to which Companies House letters and reminders will be sent. The registered office can be anywhere in England and Wales (or Scotland if your company is registered there). The registered office must always be an effective address for delivering documents to the company, and to avoid delays it is important that all correspondence sent to this address is dealt with promptly. If a company changes its registered office address after incorporation, the new address must be notified to Companies House.

What is the minimum number of officers a company requires?

Every company must have formally appointed company officers at all times. A private company must have at least:

- one director, but the company's articles of association may require more than one
- one secretary – formal qualifications are not required (a company's sole director cannot also be the company secretary).

A public company must have at least:

- two directors
- one secretary – formally qualified.

All company officers have wide responsibilities in law.

Can anyone be a company director?

In general terms, yes, but there are some rules. You can't be a company director if:

- you are an undischarged bankrupt or disqualified by a court from holding a directorship, unless given leave to act in respect of a particular company or companies
- in the case of PLCs or their subsidiaries, you are over 70 years of age or reach 70 years of age while in office, unless you are

appointed or re-appointed by resolution of the company in general meeting of which special notice has been given.

There is no minimum age limit in the Companies Act for a director to be appointed in England and Wales. However, the director must be able to consent to their own appointment. You should seek legal advice if you intend to have a very young person as a director of your company.

In Scotland the Registrar will not register for any company the appointment of a director under the age of 16 years. A child below that age does not have the legal capacity to accept a directorship – Age of Legal Capacity (Scotland) Act 1991.

Some people not of British nationality are restricted as to what work they may do while in the UK. If you need more information about whether such a person can become a director of a UK-registered company, contact: Home Office Immigration and Nationality Department on 0870 606 7766.

Can I choose any name I want for my company?

No. There are some restrictions on your choice of company name. It is important to check that the name you want is acceptable to Companies House before you complete the company formation documents.

Briefly, the restrictions are that:

- you cannot register the same name as another company;
- the use of certain words is restricted; and
- names likely to cause offence are not allowed.

It is also important to check whether your chosen name is similar to any other names already on the register. If your chosen name is too like another name, an objection could be made within the 12 months following the incorporation of your company and you could be directed by the Secretary of State to change the company's name.

Names cannot be reserved and formation applications are not processed strictly in order of time or date of receipt. If more than one application to register the same name is received, only one will be registered. The second will be refused because the name would then already be on the names index. There can be no guarantee which application will be processed first. In general, company incorporation applications delivered electronically are processed more quickly than other applications delivered on paper.

How much does Companies House charge to incorporate a company?

The standard registration fee is £20, but a premium service (£50) provides incorporation on the same day as they receive the formation documents. There is an additional fee of £15 to be paid to the Regulator when forming a community interest company. For users of the electronic filing service, the standard fee is £15 and the premium same-day service is £30. To be able to incorporate electronically, you must either purchase suitable software or develop your own. Visit www.companieshouse.gov.uk/ for more information.

Where can I obtain forms to incorporate a company?

The forms are available free of charge from Companies House but they do not provide a memorandum or articles of association.

Specimens of these documents can be obtained from legal stationers, accountants, solicitors or company formation agents. Community interest statements and excluded company declarations (only relevant for community interest companies) can be obtained from the CIC website.

PUBLIC LIMITED COMPANIES

Requirements for a PLC include the following:

- It must state that it is a public limited company both in its memorandum and in its name. The memorandum must contain a clause stating that it is a public limited company and the name must end with 'Public Limited Company' or 'PLC' (or if it is a Welsh company, the Welsh equivalents 'Cwmni Cyfyngedig Cyhoeddus' or 'CCC').
- For public limited companies that are also community interest companies (CICs), the name must end with 'community interest public limited company' or 'community interest p.l.c.' (or if it is a Welsh company, the Welsh equivalents 'cwmni buddiant cymunedol cyhoeddus cyfyngedig' or 'cwmni buddiant cymunedol c.c.c').
- The memorandum must be in the form specified.
- It must have an authorised share capital of at least £50,000.
- Before it can start business, it must have allotted shares to the value of at least £50,000. A quarter of them, £12,500, must be paid up. Each allotted share must be paid up to at least one-quarter of its nominal value together with the whole of any premium.

Can a PLC issue shares in another currency?

Yes, if it has passed the necessary resolutions to adopt that currency as part of its authorised capital and given the directors the authority to allot that capital. However, it must always have at least the authorised minimum of £50,000 sterling in issued capital, irrespective of what other currency it uses.

A company may use as many currencies as it wishes for its share capital provided that they are true currencies.

When can a PLC start business?

A newly formed PLC must not begin business or exercise any borrowing powers until it has a certificate issued under section 117 of the Companies Act 1985 confirming that the company has issued share capital of at least the statutory minimum. Once issued, the certificate is proof that the company is entitled to do business and borrow.

Do these rules apply to an overseas PLC?

Most of the above rules do not apply to a public company formed abroad. On establishing a branch or place of business in Great Britain, such a company is governed by Part XXIII of the Companies Act 1985, just as any other overseas company is. However, besides Part XXIII of the Act, they are also governed by regulations in their country of incorporation, by certain parts of the Financial Services and Markets Act 2000, and by the City Code on Take-overs and Mergers.

Details to be shown on company stationery

Under the Companies Act 1985 the company must state its name (as it appears in its memorandum of association) in certain places and on its business stationery. The company must also give certain information on all its business letters and order forms.

Every company must paint or affix its name on the outside of every office or place in which its business is carried on – even if it is a director's home. The name must be kept painted or affixed and it must be both conspicuous and legible.

The company must state its name, in legible lettering, on the following:

- all the company's business letters
- all its notices and other official publications
- all bills of exchange, promissory notes, endorsements, cheques and orders for money or goods purporting to be signed by, or on behalf of, the company
- all its bills of parcels, invoices, receipts and letters of credit.

It must also show on all its business letters and order forms its place of registration and its registered number. The place of registration must be one of the following, as appropriate:

For companies registered in England and Wales:
Registered in Cardiff
Registered in England and Wales
Registered in England
Registered in London
Registered in Wales

For companies registered in Scotland:
Registered in Scotland
Registered in Edinburgh

A company incorporated outside Great Britain which opens a branch or place of business in Great Britain must be registered and must give similar details to those stated in this chapter.

COMMUNITY INTEREST COMPANIES (CICS)

For further guidance see the CICs website at www.cicregulator.gov.uk.

ONCE YOU'RE UP AND RUNNING

The first accounts of a private company must be delivered:

- within ten months of the end of the accounting reference period, or
- if the accounting reference period is more than 12 months, within 22 months of the date of incorporation, or three months from the end of the accounting reference period, whichever is longer.

The first accounts of a public company (PLC) must be delivered:

- within seven months of the end of the accounting reference period, or
- if the accounting reference period is more than 12 months, within 19 months of the date of incorporation, or three months from the end of the accounting reference period, whichever is longer.

WHAT ELSE MUST I TELL COMPANIES HOUSE?

Here are some of the important things that you must tell them – using, in most cases, a special indexed form that they provide on their website, and within the time limits stated.

- *Changes of director(s) and secretary*, within 14 days. For:

appointments	use Form 288a
resignations	use Form 288b
change of personal details	use Form 288c

- *Details of new shares being allotted,* within one month. Use Form 88(2).
- *Any special or extraordinary resolutions and certain types of ordinary resolution,* within 15 days of them being passed by the company. There is no special form but you must send a copy of the resolution.
- When a resolution alters the memorandum or articles of association of a company, a copy of the amended document must also be sent in at the same time as the resolution.
- *Details of any mortgage or charge created by the company,* within 21 days.
- *A change of registered office,* within 14 days. Use Form 287. The change becomes legally effective only when the form has been registered.
- Deliver an annual return Form 363s to Companies House at least once every 12 months. It has 28 days from the date to which the return is made up to do this.

Filing the right forms on time is a legal requirement. If your accounts are delivered late, there is an automatic penalty. This is between £100 and £1,000 for a private company and between £500 and £5,000 for a PLC.

In addition, directors may be prosecuted for not filing certain documents. If convicted, they will have a criminal record and be liable for a fine of up to £5,000 for each offence. In some cases, they could also be disqualified from being a company director or taking part in the management of a company for up to five years.

FURTHER INFORMATION

Companies House Contact Centre staff normally provide an immediate answer to your query but if they are unable to provide an answer they will transfer you to someone who can. You can get in touch with the Companies House Contact Centre on 0870 33 33 636, or by email at enquiries@companies-house.gov.uk. Lines are open 08:30–18:00 Monday to Friday, except national holidays.

22

VAT: the basics

Value Added Tax, or VAT, is a tax that applies to most business transactions involving the transfer of goods or services. VAT is a tax on consumer expenditure. It is collected on business transactions, imports and acquisitions. And as most business transactions involve supplies of goods or services, VAT is payable if they are:

- supplies made in the United Kingdom (UK) or the Isle of Man
- by a taxable person
- in the course of a business
- are not specifically exempted or zero-rated.

There are three rates of VAT:

- a standard rate, currently 17.5%
- a reduced rate, currently 5%
- a zero rate.

Some supplies are exempt from VAT, which means that no VAT is payable. Also supplies are outside the scope of VAT if they are:

- made outside the UK and Isle of Man, or
- not made in the course of business.

REGISTERING AND CHARGING VAT

Any goods and services which are subject to VAT at any rate are called taxable supplies whether you are VAT-registered or not. If the value of your taxable supplies is over a specific limit, you need to register for VAT, unless your supplies are wholly or mainly zero rated, in which case you may apply for exemption from registration.

You may be charged a penalty if you register late and as the easiest way to register for VAT is by using the online Registration service, you need to go to the website and make sure you are complying with the necessary guidelines. Visit: customs.hmrc.gov.uk/channelsPortalWebApp/channelsPortalWebApp.portal?nfpb=true&_pageLabel=pageVAT_Home.

AFTER REGISTRATION

You need to charge VAT on all your taxable supplies from your date of registration and keep:

- a record of all standard-rated goods and services you supply or receive as part of your business
- a separate record of any exempt supplies you make
- a VAT account.

At preset intervals you need to fill in a VAT return with details of your sales and purchases. You can do this online or using a paper return. If the VAT on your sales is more than the VAT on your purchases, you pay the difference. On the other hand, if the VAT on your purchases is more than the VAT on your sales, you can claim the difference.

For small businesses, there is a flat-rate scheme that simplifies VAT accounting procedures to save time and money.

23

Childcare, schools and education

CHOOSING CHILDCARE

If you're considering childcare you have a number of options, which include:

- creches – provide occasional care for children under eight
- toddler groups – informal groups of parents and carers that meet locally with their children on a regular basis, usually including children who are under five
- preschools and playgroups – provide play time and often early education to under-fives
- day nurseries – provide care for children from birth to four or five and beyond, often integrated with early education and other services
- out-of-school or 'kids' clubs – offer children aged four to 12 a safe and stimulating environment in which they can play and learn outside school hours
- childminders – usually look after children under 12 in the childminder's own home and often collect school-aged children from a nearby school
- home childcarers – registered childminders who work in your own home (your home will need to be registered as a childcare setting if you use a home childcarer)

- nannies – provide childcare in your own home and can look after children of any age.

Finding childcare

Finding suitable childcare can be difficult but the following can help you make the right option to suit your own circumstances.

- The Childcarelink website offers comprehensive information and advice about childcare and lets you search for childcare by postcode, town and clickable map area. Visit www.direct.gov.uk.
- Your local Children's Information Service (CIS) can advise you on childcare options and availability in your area. You can get the telephone number of your nearest CIS by calling Childcarelink on freephone 0800 096 0296, or visit www.childcarelink.gov.uk/index.asp.

Ensuring childcare quality

Entrusting a stranger with your child is a big step, so before you choose childcare you should do some research. Here are some suggested options:

Ofsted registration

All childminders and daycare providers including playgroups, preschools, private nurseries, creches and out-of-school clubs for under eights, must be registered by Ofsted (the Office for Standards in Education). Ofsted registers these providers and makes sure they meet the national standards for under-eights' day care and child-minding, and ensures that all those who work with children are fit to do so. Ofsted also checks that the environment provided for children is secure and safe.

Childcarelink

You can check if a childcare provider is registered by asking to see a registration certificate. If you have any doubts about a provider, check with your local Children's Information Service. You can get the telephone number of your nearest CIS by calling Childcarelink on 0800 096 0296, or visit www.childcarelink.gov.uk/index.asp.

Ofsted inspection reports

These reports provide detailed information on individual childcare providers (except for childminders), based on Ofsted's annual inspections. Visit www.ofsted.gov.uk/ and search for inspection reports using your own postcode.

Do your own research

It is always a good idea to visit childcare providers yourself – inspections and accreditation are no substitute for your own judgement. When you do visit, ask plenty of questions. If you're thinking of employing a nanny, bear in mind that government-sponsored registration and accreditation schemes do not apply to them. It is up to you, as parent and employer, to make sure that you hire a nanny who will look after your children well.

Reporting childcare concerns and complaints

If you have a concern or complaint you can't resolve with your registered childcare provider, although Ofsted does not usually become involved in complaints over fees and contractual arrangements, you can call Ofsted's Early Years Complaints helpline on 0845 601 47 72.

Help with childcare costs

Childcare can be expensive, so it's worth checking to see if you qualify for any help. But be aware that all government programmes that provide help with childcare costs require you to use Ofsted-registered childcare. Visit www.direct.gov.uk.

Free early years education for three- and four-year-olds

If your child is three or four, they are entitled to free early years education at a registered provider. This includes five sessions a week, two and a half hours per day, for three terms each year. Your local Children's Information Service (CIS) can advise you on availability in your area. You can get the number of your nearest CIS by calling 0800 096 0296 or visit www.childcarelink.gov.uk/index.asp.

OVERVIEW OF THE EDUCATION SYSTEM

There are different types of school and methods of application when choosing a school for your child. As a UK citizen, your child is entitled to a free education up to the age of 16 years (compulsory school age), or to the age of 18 years with added sixth-form education. UK schools will welcome your children, whatever their faith or nationality. Multi-faith assemblies in primary and secondary schools are commonplace and children are taught to respect each other's beliefs.

Primary schools

Your child's first day at 'real school' is a big step, and from now on their life outside home will develop daily. New experiences will help your child grow and become independent, underpinned by your own active support.

These years are crucial for reading, the one skill which children need in order to access the rest of their education successfully. The importance of reading outside school is continually being stressed by educationalists and psychologists. To help you develop your child using the UK system that's available, there are some useful tips and guidance available from the government via its website, www.direct.gov.uk/EducationAndLearning.

Preparing your child for school life

If children have a good idea of what school is going to be like and have practised the skills needed there, they're less likely to find the experience stressful. You can build your child's confidence by taking a positive approach:

- explain where they'll be going and for how long
- answer questions, and iron out wrong impressions by asking what they think it might be like
- turn-taking games and little role-plays at home can help your child get into the right frame of mind
- practise the practical things – coping with coats and shoes, and opening lunchbox items like yoghurts and drinks
- don't dismiss your child's fears – things that are obvious or silly to grown-ups can seem like terrible obstacles to a five-year-old.

What your child will learn

The first two years of primary school are called Key Stage 1, and the next four are Key Stage 2. For each of these stages, the government has put in place a teaching framework called the National Curriculum which lays down which subjects are taught at every school. For more information on the National Curriculum, see below.

Homework

All schools have their own homework policies, and you can request a copy so you can see what your child should be doing. Some schools make sure parents are aware of homework by asking them to sign a homework book.

Out-of-school arrangements

Breakfast clubs and after-school clubs are available at many schools and offer parents or carers the chance to leave children and collect them outside ordinary school hours. Individual schools or the ChildcareLink freephone service on 0800 096 0296 can give you more information, or visit www.childcarelink.gov.uk/index.asp.

Home education

In the UK, parents do not have to send their children to school, but the law does require that children are educated.

SUCCESSFUL SCHOOLS

Since 1994/95, the UK government has measured schools' performance through annual inspections and the publishing of an annual report which shows, every year, which schools have achieved 'successful school' status.

Up to and including 2003/04, some 2,669 schools and 65 colleges have been identified as particularly successful.

Schools are considered 'successful' on the basis of:

- the judgements in the schools' inspection report, in particular those relating to overall effectiveness (since January 2000), the quality of teaching, leadership and management, and improvement since the last inspection

- the attainment of the schools' pupils in national tests and exams; in both cases the selection takes into account the particular circumstances of schools
- for colleges, they should be very well led and provide a consistently high standard of education and training for their students.

For more information visit www.ofsted.gov.uk/ and select the 'successful schools' link.

UNDERSTANDING THE NATIONAL CURRICULUM FOR ENGLAND

The National Curriculum sets out the stages and core subjects your child will be taught throughout their school life. Children aged five to 16 in state or maintained schools must be taught according to the National Curriculum. Knowing the stages and subjects that make up the National Curriculum is important.

National Curriculum subjects

The National Curriculum, taught to all pupils, is made up of modules, known as key stages. It is organised on the basis of four key stages, as shown on page 202.

Schools don't have to use these titles for subjects, and some subjects can also be taught together under one name, as long as the National Curriculum is covered. For more about the National Curriculum for England, visit www.nc.uk.net.

Teachers assess children against the National Curriculum levels regularly as they learn. You'll receive information about the level

	Key stage 1	Key stage 2	Key stage 3	Key stage 4	
Age	5–7	7–11	11–14	14–16	
Year groups	1–2	3–6	7–9	10–11	
English	■	■	■	■	National Curriculum core subjects
Mathematics	■	■	■	■	
Science	■	■	■	■	
Design and technology	■	■	■		National Curriculum non-core foundation subjects
Information and communication technology	■	■	■	■	
History	■	■	■		
Geography	■	■	■		
Modern foreign languages			■		
Art and design	■	■	■		
Music	■	■	■		
Physical education	■	■	■	■	
Citizenship			■	■	
Religious education	■	■	■	■	
Careers education			■	■	
Sex education			■	■	
Work-related learning				■	
Personal, social and health education	□	□	□	□	

■ Statutory
□ Non-statutory

your child has reached at parent–teacher evenings and in their school reports.

The National Curriculum key stage tests

At the end of each key stage there are national tests. Children can't 'fail' these tests. They are intended to show if a child is working above or below the target levels for their age, so that the right plans can be made for their future learning. They also allow schools to see whether they are teaching effectively, by looking at their pupils' performance against national results.

Key Stage 1 tests for seven-year-olds have two elements, teacher assessment and written tests, in reading, writing (including handwriting), spelling and maths. The tests are spread out, and altogether they last for less than three hours.

Key Stage 2 tests for 11-year-olds also comprise teacher assessment and written elements. The written tests cover:

- English – reading, writing (including handwriting) and spelling
- mathematics (including mental arithmetic)
- science.

These tests are held in mid-May, and altogether they last less than five-and-a-half hours.

CHOOSING SCHOOLS

State schools

These schools are funded entirely from government money and are found in all towns. They are open to all children regardless of race, religion or beliefs. The different kinds of state school are:

- community schools provided by the local education authority, which is responsible for admissions

- foundation schools provided by a foundation or trust and for which the governing body is responsible for admissions

- voluntary schools provided by a foundation or trust; most voluntary schools have a religious character and are known as faith schools.

If you have a firm faith you may find a faith school that you would like your child to attend. It may be farther away from your home but the local education authority may be able to help with travel. If the school is voluntary aided you will need to approach the school directly about its admissions criteria. For voluntary controlled faith schools the local education authority is responsible for admissions.

Independent (private) schools

Parents may choose to pay for their child's education at an independent school. These schools are funded privately. Parents usually pay fees annually in advance and are expected to be able to pay for the duration of the school (i.e. in secondary school for the whole four years). Rates vary so it's best to talk to the school directly about their fees. Confusingly, independent schools in England and Wales are often called 'public schools'.

School uniform

The governing body of each school decides on the uniform policy or dress code, and it is the headteacher's responsibility to make sure pupils keep to the rules. If you have any complaints about the uniform policy or dress code, talk to the school's governing body.

Cost of school uniform

When deciding on a uniform policy, all schools are expected to consider cost. No school uniform should be so expensive as to leave pupils or their families feeling excluded.

The government believes it is unacceptable for the cost of a uniform to stop parents from sending their child to the school of their choice. Governing bodies should consult parents for their views and concerns before changing or deciding on a new uniform policy.

Physical education (PE)

School uniform often includes clothing required for PE lessons. Schools are supposed to choose a PE kit which is practical, comfortable and appropriate to the activity involved. Sex and race discrimination issues must also be considered. As with the regular school uniform, school governing bodies are expected to consider the cost to parents when deciding on a policy for PE kit.

Breaching uniform policy

If your child breaks the rules when it comes to school uniform, they could be punished by the headteacher. More serious punishments like suspension or expulsion from the school are only considered acceptable if the pupil's behaviour has been generally defiant in other areas as well.

Schools should be considerate if a pupil does not keep to the uniform policy, and try to find out why it is happening. If a family is having financial difficulties, the school should allow for this and give the parents time to buy the right items.

Cultural, race and religious requirements

While pupils must stick to the school's uniform policy, UK schools must be considerate to the needs of different cultures, races and religions.

Sex discrimination issues

Schools should ensure that their uniform policy does not

discriminate on the grounds of gender. For example, girls should normally be allowed to wear trousers. Uniform rules should not disadvantage one gender compared with the other.

SCHOOL TERM DATES AND HOLIDAYS

The dates for school terms and holidays are decided by the local education authority (LEA) or the governing body of a school. Some LEAs have introduced a year with six terms, each of similar length. However, for the majority of schools the current school year is divided into three terms. To locate your LEA, go to: www.dfes.gov.uk/leagateway/index.cfm?action=address.default.

The following is intended as a rough guide only to term dates. For exact details please contact the LEA or school in your area.

Academic year 2006–2007

Autumn term

Autumn Half Term: from 23 October 2006 to 27 October 2006
Christmas Holidays: from 20 December 2006 to 02 January 2007

Spring term

Spring Half Term: from 19 February 2007 to 23 February 2007
Easter Holiday: from 02 April 2007 to 13 April 2007

Summer term

Summer Half Term: from 28 May 2007 to 01 June 2007
Summer Holiday: from 23 July 2007 to 31 August 2007

Holidays during school term time

The following advice is provided on the 'Education and learning' section of the Directgov website, direct.gov.uk. You should not normally take your child on holiday in term time as it can be disruptive both to your child's education and to the school.

Holidays in term time can only be agreed by the headteacher or someone with appropriate authority at their discretion. They can only agree to more than ten school days' absence in any school year in exceptional circumstances. You should discuss proposed holidays with the school before you book them. Each holiday request will be treated individually and the following will be taken into consideration:

- the time of year for the proposed trip
- if it's near any exam dates
- your child's overall attendance pattern
- any holidays already taken in the school year
- the age and stage of education of your child.
- your wishes.

COLLEGES AND UNIVERSITIES

Universities and colleges in the UK are increasingly international. When you study here, you are likely to find yourself meeting students from all over the world. More than 90 countries may be represented on campus and each student makes a unique contribution to the life of the institution, both academically and culturally.

This internationalism is demonstrated by student societies established within students' unions, where those centred on religious or geographical themes are numerous.

Colleges and universities make an effort to meet international students' dietary and religious needs. Vegetarian dishes are served daily in university canteens. Single-sex accommodation is usually available on campus on request. Universities pride themselves on giving students the freedom to worship and practise their religion; prayer areas and chapels for all the major religions of the world are easily accessible.

If you are staying in private accommodation, you should tell your hosts of any customs that you wish them to respect while you are staying with them. For example, if there are certain foods that you may not eat or if you need some privacy every day to pray or meditate, explain these needs to your hosts and ask for their co-operation.

If you are moving to the UK and have finished school, you will find some useful information on further education, including postgraduate study, in Chapter 9.

Relevant websites

http://www.aimhigher.ac.uk/universities___colleges___hei/index.cfm. Allows you to view institutions in specific areas across the UK. Also offers advice about student financing and how to apply.

www.direct.gov.uk/EducationAndLearning/UniversityAndHigherEducation/. How to apply for a college or university placement once you've qualified from a UK school.

(24)

Housing

BACKPACKER AND STUDENT HOUSING IN LONDON

Unless you have mates, or mates of mates, to stay with, you will need to look at short-term accommodation until you get established. If your main goal is to start a job in the UK quickly after you arrive, you should plan to find a short-term, well located, reasonably priced, safe and secure place to stay in when you first arrive. There are lots of accommodation options in and some types are far more suited to some than others.

- **Backpacker hostels in London** – Traditionally the way to getting backpacker accommodation in London is through a hostel. Hostels are relatively inexpensive and a great way to meet lots of travellers. Cleanliness and comfort and privacy levels vary between the different London hostels so it pays to shop around. Visit www.workgateways.com for a list of hostels. Also see http://www.tntmag.co.uk/ and www.gumtree.com.

- **Staying at a guest house, small hotel or bed and breakfast**. For the working traveller, in terms of privacy and a safe place for your belongings, you may want to consider the above rather than a hostel. In most guest houses or small hotels you will probably have your own room; however, you may have to share a bathroom with several other guests. If you can share a twin room with a mate, you will find it even cheaper. Safes for your valuables are sometimes provided. Hot breakfasts are usually included and you'll have a cupboard in which to hang your job-searching suit. If you go out of peak season or decide to stay longer-term, many UK guest houses and small hotels will offer a discount if you ask.

- **Shared accommodation**. Visit www.accommodationlondon.net and you will find a range of studio apartments and shared houses in London which are fully equipped and accessible. They are usually in demand so you need to act quickly.

- **Live-in accommodation in the UK**. Many jobs within a pub or hotel environment such as waiting tables, bartending, reception and chef jobs provide live-in work arrangements. Often in a live-in arrangement some meals and board are included and depending on the number of hours you work you can be paid wages on top of this. Live-in work is more often found outside London, in regional UK areas, smaller cities and towns.

TYPES OF LONGER-TERM ACCOMMODATION

- **Flats** are generally apartments with one to three or more bedrooms which are to be let, or rented, as an entire unit.

- **Flat-shares** come available when a flat is already occupied and one or more bedrooms become available for rent. This means you'll be sharing common facilities of the flat such as kitchen, lounge room and usually bathroom.

- **Bed-sits** are interesting and popular in the UK. Usually an old multi-level house will be split up into mini-apartments. This mini-apartment will generally just be a bedroom with perhaps some room for a sitting area; sometimes there are sinks in the bedrooms as well. Bathroom and kitchen facilities are generally shared with either all those in the house, or just tenants on the same floor. This can be an inexpensive and convenient accommodation option. It's a hybrid between a guest house and renting a flat.

- **Houses** can be rented but are harder to find and extremely expensive in London. They are more easily found in regional UK areas.

BEFORE RENTING IN THE UK – ADDITIONAL COSTS AND CONSIDERATIONS

- **Location**. Different boroughs (suburbs or neighbourhoods) in London and the UK have a different lifestyle and price associated with them. So research your chosen location well before you move so you know what to expect.

- **Transportation links**. Before signing a lease anywhere, you should be sure to walk to the nearest transportation links, catch the bus, train or tube at rush hour and see how long it takes you to get to other key areas. In general, though, walking proximity to a Tube or British Rail station is highly sought after. A bus stop nearby is the next best thing.

- **Furnishings**. Most UK flats and homes are rented furnished, with basics. If a flat is advertised as furnished, be sure to determine exactly what is provided. If something is in a particularly poor state, ask to have it replaced; it is the landlord's responsibility to provide the basics, in good repair, in a furnished flat.

- **Bond**. Most, if not all, rental arrangements will require you to pay a bond, which is usually equivalent to a full month's rent. You will usually get this bond back after you have moved out and the place has been inspected.

- **Estate or letting agencies**. Unless you find flat-shares through friends, or magazines and websites, most of the ads for flat rentals in the newspaper are through estate, or letting, agents. Agents have shops across the UK and they should be able to offer you advice, ideas and information on what they have available. Some agents have better reputations than others but as long as you ask questions and read your lease very carefully you should have a good experience.

- **Flat mates**. Can make living in London, and other major cities, affordable and fun. Often people at your work will know someone with a room available. In general you should not have a problem finding an affordable location. One word of advice: if you are signing a lease for a three-bedroom flat, you should try to be sure that you have three people ready to move in who are planning to stay for the duration of the lease. Assuming you will always be able to find someone suitable to fill up the flat can lead to headaches and financial distress.
- **Council Tax** is a compulsory tax levied by the local government or borough council and is paid by all residents of that borough or neighbourhood. When you sign a lease and rent a flat, be sure you have received all the information on the Council Tax due for that property. The Council Tax invoice will be posted to your address and it is to be paid by those who have signed the lease. Budget about £50+ per person per month depending on your area.
- **Heating/electricity**. Be sure to find out how the flat is heated. Electric heating is expensive and is therefore not ideal. Some flats and houses have gas central heating. Beware of renting a flat that shares a heating system with other flats as you lose some usage and cost control of the heating. Gas and electricity could be around £50 per month as a general budget figure.

- **Water**. Water utility charges vary from area to area, but you need to allow around £20 per month.

- **TV licence**. The UK requires all those who own a TV to pay for a TV licence. An annual colour TV Licence costs £131.50 and a black-and-white licence costs £44.00. Detection of non-licence payers is intense and the fines are huge. Contact www.tvlicensing.co.uk/ to organise payment.

- **Telephone**. Many people prefer to use a mobile phone rather than get a landline for their flat. This is a great idea if you are sharing your accommodation as it saves arguments over the phone bills. If you want a landline you will need British Telecom (BT) to install it (at an additional cost) and it will then cost you around £12 per month standing charge plus calls; www.bt.com.

DECIDING WHERE TO LIVE

Research is the best way of finding somewhere suitable to live. You need to consider your own circumstances in order to find a location that will be suitable, either in the short or longer term. You need to consider things like:

- where you are most likely to find work or be located for work
- the type of schools/colleges, etc. required for your children
- accessibility to travel to work, e.g. public transport
- social aspects of the neighbourhood you require
- local amenities.

Once you are clear about your own needs, research using the Internet, scan national and local UK newspapers and watch local regional UK TV news programmes (usually accessed through satellite TV channels) to give you a flavour of different UK areas.

For easy to access maps of the whole UK, visit www.streetmap.co.uk. To find out about a local area, start with the local tourist information centres. For England visit www.visitengland.com/; for Scotland visit www.visitscotland.com/; and for Wales visit www.visitwales.com/. Also visit www.rightmove.co.uk/home.rsp – they can provide you with a list of your local rental and buying agents anywhere in the UK and at the same time you can also search the accommodation that they have currently available.

BUYING OR RENTING

Buying or renting a house really depends on whether you know exactly where you want to be and have a cash deposit to put down on a property, in which case buying could be an ideal option. Or maybe you are still undecided about location, job, schools, etc., so want to get to know an area before you make roots, in which case renting could be for you.

BUYING A HOUSE

In most cases mortgage lenders require you to put down at least a 5 per cent deposit based on the price of the house, before they will provide you the 95 per cent financing on the remainder of the price. So if the house you plan to buy is £100,000 you need a £5,000 cash deposit as a minimum. There are some lenders who will provide 100 per cent mortgages but you will pay higher interest repayments as a result, if you qualify. To find some good deals on mortgages and other finance options, visit www.thisismoney.co.uk. Also have a look at www.moneysupermarket.com where you can compare prices on mortgages, loans and lots of other financial stuff. If you are not sure about financial products, you may like to visit www.unbiased.co.uk where you will find a list of independent financial advisors operating in your area.

Other costs to consider

You pay Stamp Duty Land Tax on property like houses, flats, other buildings and land. This can be a hefty cost to add onto the cost of buying your house, and can't be overlooked.

Cost of property vs Stamp Duty Rate

	Rate of Duty
Up to and including £60,000, provided a certificate of value for £60,000 is included in the document	nil
Over £60,000 but not more than £250,000, provided a certificate of value for £250,000 is included in the document	1%
Over £250,000 but not more than £500,000, provided a certificate of value for £500,000 is included in the document	3%
Over £500,000	4%

You will also need to factor in solicitors' conveyancing charges which vary considerably depending on where your solicitor is located and where your home is located. To find an approved solicitor by the Law Society, visit www.lawsociety.org.uk/choosingandusing/findasolicitor.law.

Research

As with most major purchases, make sure you shop around. The local newspapers provide local ads about property for sale and the Internet also offers lots of opportunities to see what's on the market. In all towns and cities you will find estate agents, where you can call in and register to be sent property details or just call in and make arrangements to view something you've seen advertised. All estate agents place 'For Sale' boards in front of the properties they are selling, with their office telephone number clearly visible.

The Internet also provides a convenient option when searching for property. At www.rightmove.co.uk you can research different areas of the UK and search what properties are for sale. They even provide you with a list of all the estate agents in all areas of the UK.

Property prices

The cost of property has escalated considerably in recent years. In London you can expect to pay around £250,000 for a one-bedroom flat that's quite centrally located. Obviously the further out of central London you live, the cheaper it is and the more you buy for your money.

In most other major UK cities prices are greater than in outlying areas. The only exception is for idyllic country properties that usually tend to sell at premium prices – but again, the further from London they are, generally you get an awful lot more for your money.

Estate agents

The following advice is provided on the 'Home and community' section of the Directgov website, www.direct.gov.uk. Whether buying or selling, you will probably use the services of an estate agent. Although they don't need to be registered to set up in business, many do belong to the National Association of Estate Agents (NAEA) and the Ombudsman for Estate Agents (OEA).

Choosing and working with an estate agent

You may want to choose an estate agent that is registered with the NAEA or the Ombudsman, as this will mean they have to abide by a code of practice. You can find one in the area in which you are interested by searching on the NAEA website. All estate agents are bound by the Estate Agents Act, whether or not they are registered with a governing body.

Useful sites include the following:

- Estate Agents Act – www.oft.gov.uk/Business/Legal/Estate/default.htm
- the Office of Fair Trading (OFT): Using an estate agent to buy or sell your home booklet – www.naea.co.uk/the_naea/
- National Association of Estate Agents – www.naea.co.uk/the_naea/
- Ombudsman for Estate Agents – www.oea.co.uk/.

Making an offer on a property

If you make an offer on a property, make sure that it is 'subject to contract'; this means you can pull out of the deal if there are any problems. Under the Estate Agents Act, an estate agent is legally bound to present any offer to the vendor.

Unlike in Scotland, a buyer's offer is not legally binding in England and Wales, even if accepted by the seller.

Once your offer is accepted, ask for the property to be taken straight off the market for the duration of the sale. The seller may be reluctant to do this if you haven't already sold your property. There is a risk that another determined buyer may go straight to the seller with a higher offer.

Exchanging and completing contracts

In England and Wales, contracts are drawn up between the buyer and seller. This whole process from the point of making an offer, receiving your mortgage acceptance and having all the necessary surveys and searches completed on the property can take a minimum of six weeks. However, be prepared that it may take longer. To ensure a degree of certainty to the sale, many agree to exchange contracts before they actually complete the contractual process.

To exchange contracts you normally pay 5 per cent or 10 per cent of the property price and legally sign a document to finish the legal contract completion within a fixed period of days. In some cases, people prefer to exchange and complete contracts on the same day so that the property becomes legally theirs at the same time as the money is paid in full.

RENTING

If you are not sure where to be based or if you like where you are planning to be based, renting is probably your best option. Rental costs vary across the UK, but there tends to be more rental accommodation in London than any other city in the UK. Typically the sort of prices you can expect to pay in London are as follows.

London cost of accommodation

Average flat-share rental per month		Average one-bedroom flat rental per month	
East London	£400	East London	£600
West London	£500	West London	£700
South London	£400	South London	£600
North London	£500	North London	£700

For the rest of the UK, city rentals will be more expensive than more outlying areas but you'll get more for your money. In more urban areas there tends to be less property to rent, as most people buy. However, it is always worth shopping around to see what you can get for the money you want to spend.

Most accommodation in the UK is furnished, which usually includes living room, bedroom and kitchen furniture and items (usually including fridge, oven, washing machine) or even a dishwasher.

Properties tend to come in studio, one-bed, two-bed, three-bed flats. Detached or semi-detached houses (which are usually hard to find in London) are popular in other areas of the country as they offer space and more privacy than flats.

Signing up and costs

When you've found a place you want to rent, you will be asked for several references and perhaps even interviewed before you will be accepted as a suitable tenant for your chosen property.

The rental agents or landlord will take a full inventory of the items at the property and a copy of the tenancy contract will be given to you. In most cases it is worth having it checked by a solicitor just to make sure you are getting what you agreed to. Once you are happy, you sign the contract, and your tenancy begins from the agreed date.

You will be expected to pay the first month's rent in advance and usually about six weeks' rent as a deposit. Some rental agencies will also charge you a fee for signing up, so check with each agent before you sign anything.

Other relevant contacts include:

- www.gumtree.co.uk
- www.letdirect.com
- Flatfinder 020 7243 5544
- www.rightmove.co.uk.

Healthcare

ABOUT THE NHS

The NHS was set up in 1948 and is now the largest organisation in Europe and is recognised as one of the best health services in the world by the World Health Organisation.

Department of Health

This is the department that supports the government in improving the health and well-being of the population. The Department of Health started a programme of change in 2005, designed to make sure they provide leadership to the NHS and social care.

Making changes to the NHS

The 'Shifting the Balance of Power' programme has been introduced by the government and aims to design a service centred on patients, which puts them first. It aims to be faster, more convenient and offer more choice than in the past.

The main feature of the change has been to give locally based groups called Primary Care Trusts (PCTs) the role of running the NHS and improving health in their areas. This has also led to new Strategic Health Authorities being created which cover larger areas and now take a more strategic role.

NHS services

Primary care is the first point of contact most people have with the NHS and is delivered by a wide range of professionals, including family GPs, nurses, dentists, pharmacists and opticians.

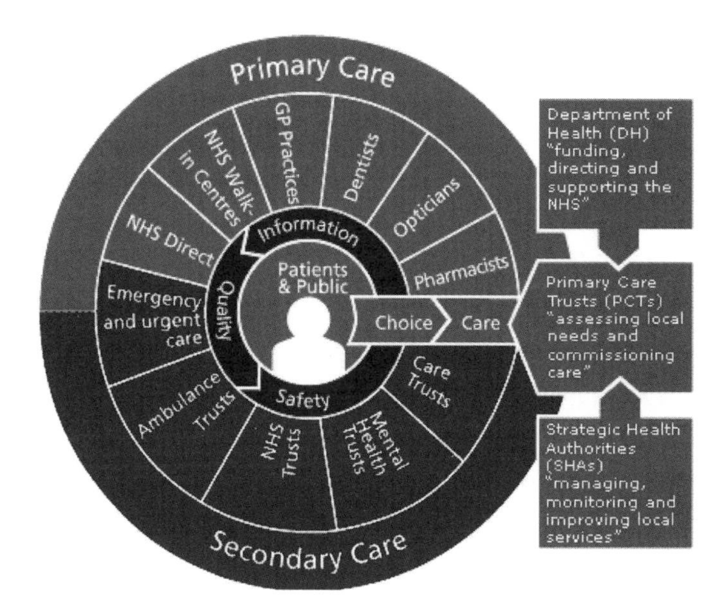

This care focuses on the treatment of routine injuries and illnesses as well as preventive care, such as services to help people stop smoking. Primary care is mostly concerned with a patient's general health needs, but increasingly more specialist treatments and services are becoming available in primary care settings closer to where people live.

ABOUT NHS DIRECT ONLINE AND THE NHS DIRECT TELEPHONE SERVICE

The NHS Direct Online's health information enquiry service is intended for use if you cannot find the health information you need on the NHS Direct Online website. They aim to respond to all enquiries within up to five working days from receipt of your enquiry but if your enquiry is more urgent, the NHS offer a telephone service called NHS Direct on 0845 4647.

The information you submit to NHS Direct Online will be treated in the strictest confidence. Your enquiry will be researched by a skilled health information professional, who will provide you with an individual response. The information you supply and the response provided will be stored securely by NHS Direct Online for at least five years.

NHS Direct Online's health information enquiry service only provides information about named health conditions. The service doesn't provide diagnoses, advice or counselling and is only available to residents in England. So if you begin to feel ill, it is best to call NHS Direct immediately to get a nurse's advice.

NHS WALK-IN CENTRES

NHS walk-in centres offer fast and convenient access to a range of NHS services, including health information, advice and treatment for a range of minor illnesses (coughs, colds, infections) and minor injuries (strains, sprains, cuts).

Most centres are open from early morning to late evening, seven days a week. The centres are run by experienced NHS nurses, and you don't need to make an appointment. You should be aware that some newly opened centres may offer different opening hours during the first few months.

These centres are helping to improve the way in which thousands of patients get immediate treatment for troublesome minor health problems or injuries. To find your nearest centre, visit www.nhs.uk/England/NoAppointmentNeeded/WalkInCentres/.

EMERGENCY SERVICES

Emergency Services in the UK are accessed by calling one telephone number, 999. The call is free from any phone and you will be asked whether you require the services of Police, Fire or Ambulance.

REGISTERING WITH A DOCTOR (COMMONLY KNOWN AS GPs – GENERAL PRACTITIONERS)

GPs assess patients, provide preventative advice, prescribe medication and refer patients to other specialists. They may also provide contraception advice, sexual health services, maternity care and vaccinations. All GPs have a contract to provide a 24-hour service. These may include a GP out-of-hours call-out service or out-of-hours drop-in clinics that enable patients to visit without an appointment. During normal daytime hours, most GPs work on an appointment-only basis.

You can register with a GP by looking up your local practice and providing them with your medical card details. If you do not have a medical card you should fill in form GMS1, which should be available at the surgery. Once you have been accepted as a patient, your medical records will be transferred to the new surgery and you will be sent a new medical card. When you register with a new GP it is a good idea to ask for an information leaflet about the surgery and its services and policies.

There are a number of reasons why you may not be able to register with your chosen GP. For example, the practice may be full or you may live too far away. If this is the case, simply choose another GP in your local area.

If you have difficulty registering with a GP, the local PCT will be able to help. You can get the number from the phone book: look under Health Services in the A–Z listing of local businesses and services. You can also get the number from NHS Direct on 0845 4647 or from the NHS websites (details of which are shown at the end of this chapter).

You can register with a GP on a permanent or temporary basis. If you are ill and travelling through the area for three months or less, you can register with a GP as a temporary patient. If you stay for longer than three months, you can permanently register with that GP if they are prepared to take you on.

FINDING A GP, DENTIST, OPTICIAN OR PHARMACY

The NHS websites (all shown below) allows you to search for your five nearest GPs, opticians, dentists and pharmacies. All you have to do is put in your postcode and it does the rest for you.

PRESCRIPTIONS

Prescriptions are issued by GPs and prescription charges apply to everyone except:

- children under the age of 16
- young people under the age of 19 and in full-time education
- people over the age of 60
- people who suffer from a specific range of conditions.

Some other people may also be entitled to help with medical charges, such as those who qualify for the NHS Low Income Scheme. The NHS also provides a prescription pre-payment scheme, which enables patients who require repeat prescriptions to purchase prepaid certificates (PPCs).

All the information you require about prescriptions and GP services is available through the various NHS websites, details of which are shown below.

ALL THE CONTACTS YOU NEED

NHS telephone services

- NHS Direct – 0845 46 47

  A 24-hour nurse-led advice service for England, Wales and Northern Ireland.

- NHS 24 – 08454 24 24 24

  In Scotland, NHS 24 provides a health advice and support service.

- NHS Direct Wales/Galw Iechyd Cymru – 0845 46 47 also caters for Welsh speakers. There is also a separate website for NHS Direct Wales with information in English and Welsh.

NHS online services

- www.nhs.uk/ the main gateway to all the NHS services in the UK
- www.nhsdirect.nhs.uk/ NHS for England
- www.n-i.nhs.uk/ NHS in Northern Ireland
- www.show.scot.nhs.uk/ NHS in Scotland
- www.wales.nhs.uk/ NHS in Wales
- The Isle of Man and the Channel Islands have separate independent health service structures. For more information please visit the Isle of Man Government, States of Guernsey Government www.gov.im/dhss/health/ and States of Jersey Government www.health.gov.je/.

PRIVATE HEALTH SCHEMES

What's good about private medical cover?

The main reason most people choose to go private is that they want to avoid NHS waiting lists. They also want to choose their specialist; have more flexible visiting times; a private room; and better quality meals.

What's bad about private medical cover?

It's very expensive, particularly if you want a good comprehensive policy, and premiums rise the older you get, although a few companies do not penalise you for getting older – so make sure you shop around.

Can you obtain private cover through your job?

Some jobs already provide employees with private medical insurance; others may offer it at a subsidised rate. This is well worth taking up and you may also be able to buy discounted cover for your partner and any children.

Do not expect cover for existing health problems

Insurance is there for the unknown. This means any existing health condition will be excluded. Some existing conditions may become insurable after a waiting period set by the insurer, provided the condition does not reoccur during this period.

Which insurer to choose?

Do not just pick a big-name insurer. There are smaller ones that offer very good service and cover. All insurance companies based in the UK and offering insurance are regulated, so you can buy with confidence.

Cash plans

A cash plan pays out a set amount if you need to go into hospital, also for other healthcare needs such as glasses. Paid by regular subscription, these plans have benefits and can top up your income, but they are not a substitute for insurance.

If you want to find private medical health cover, shop around on the Internet. Sites such as www.thisismoney.co.uk/health and www.moneysupermarket.com all offer a facility for you to compare policies.

26

Transport

DRIVING IN THE UK

As one of the quartet of trillion-dollar economies of Western Europe, the road network in the UK is a mass of motorways, expressways and smaller roads. A total of 392,931 km of roads assist the population to get around with relative ease, although congestion does occur at peak times in the morning and evening in particular. Around the many tourist hotspots the roads get jammed easily so if you are planning to drive, allow extra time and check out the travel reports. Live traffic updates are available 24 hours a day by calling 08700 660 115. The local radio and TV stations also carry travel bulletins throughout the day.

Driving licences

If you already hold a driving licence you may be able to use it for up to 12 months before you will be required to take a UK driving test. Alternatively you may be able to swap your existing licence for a British licence or apply for a provisional licence and then take a test.

The DVLA is the UK agency that manages all driving licence-related enquiries. Their website is www.dvla.gov.uk. For international students needing advice on driving licences, a complete selection of guidance notes is available to download from: www.ukcosa.org.uk/pages/guidenote.htm.

Rules of the road

- Drive on the left-hand side of the road.

- Give priority to traffic coming from the right.
- Pass on the outside (right) lane.
- Do not pass on the inside (left) lane.
- Do not block the middle lane if the inside lane is clear.
- When approaching a roundabout, give priority to traffic approaching from the right, unless otherwise indicated.
- At a junction there is no general priority rule, as priority is marked at most junctions. On a minor road you will see either a triangular 'GIVE WAY' or red 'STOP' sign. Many junctions will have only 'GIVE WAY' markings on the carriageway (dotted white lines and a white triangle on the carriageway). These signs must be obeyed.
- All vehicles must give way to emergency services vehicles.
- The use of a car horn is not permitted in built-up areas from 23:30 to 07:00 hours.

Drinking and driving

Alcohol can have a serious affect on judgement and your ability to drive. The legal limit is 80mg of alcohol per 100ml of blood, or 35 microgrammes of alcohol to 100ml of breath. There are severe penalties for driving while under the influence of alcohol and a big anti-drink and drive campaign operates in the UK.

Car accidents

If you are involved in an accident you must stop. Give details of your insurance to other drivers involved. If anyone is injured, you must also inform the police using the emergency number **999**.

Emergencies on motorways

Orange emergency telephones are situated at approximately half-mile intervals along motorways. They connect the caller to the Police

Motorway Control Centre, who can send the appropriate help, e.g. to breakdown recovery companies such as the AA (www.theaa.com), RAC (www.rac.co.uk), or the police, ambulance or fire brigade.

Special warning signals

Special warning signals are used on motorways to warn drivers of danger ahead. The panels are situated either on the central reservation or above each lane. On urban motorways, the signals are overhead, one for each lane.

Seatbelts

All new cars must have front and rear seatbelts fitted. A car which was not obliged to have seatbelts fitted at the time it was first used does not need to have them fitted now. But if they are fitted they must be worn. For children under 14, it is the responsibility of the driver to ensure appropriate restraint is worn.

Mobile phones

It is an offence to use a mobile phone while driving. Offenders will be fined £30 initially, rising to a maximum of £1,000 if their case goes to court. Those caught breaking the ban will also get three penalty points on their licence for each offence. Under current laws, motorists can only be prosecuted for using mobiles if they fail to keep proper control of their vehicle.

Speed limits

- Built-up areas: all vehicles, 30 mph (48 kph).
- Single carriageway: 60 mph (96 kph) for cars, 50 mph (81 kph) for cars towing caravans or trailers, buses and coaches.
- Dual Carriageways/Motorways: 70 mph (112 kph) for cars, 60 mph (96 kph) for cars towing caravans or trailers.

Note: the maximum speed limits in Jersey and Guernsey are 40 mph (65 kph) and 35 mph (56 kph) respectively.

LONDON CONGESTION CHARGE

The Congestion Charge is a £8 daily charge to drive in central London at certain times. Congestion charging was introduced on 17 February 2003 by the Mayor of London and is designed to reduce traffic congestion by encouraging people to use public transport. The money raised is being used to improve public transport in London.

The congestion charging zone operates across eight square miles in the centre of London. A westward extension to the zone is due to become operational in 2007. To check which roads are in the zone, view the Congestion Charge map located at: www.cclondon.com/infosearch/dynamicPages/WF_ZoneCheck_W.aspx. The zone operates between 07:00 and 18:30, Monday to Friday. There is no charge at weekends or on Public Holidays.

Once you've paid £8 each day to go into the London congestion zone area, you can enter and leave as many time as you like. The charge can be paid on a daily or weekly basis and you can also pay it up to 90 days before you arrive in London. All payments must be in UK currency.

You don't have to pay before you drive into the zone but you must pay before 22:00 that day to avoid penalty charges. The zone is monitored by cameras, which record all vehicle number plates and determine whether the charge has been paid. They recognise both British and European number plates.

The easiest way to pay is at www.cclondon.com or by phone on +44 (0) 20 7649 9122 – Minicom +44 (0) 20 7649 9123 using credit or debit cards. MasterCard and Visa cards are accepted – American Express and Diners Club aren't.

You'll need to provide your vehicle registration number, the date(s) you would like to pay the charge for, and your credit/debit card details. Keep a note of the receipt number as your proof of payment. You can also pay at special self-service machines in major car parks, at selected petrol stations and at shops displaying the congestion charging sign.

If you don't pay the charge, the penalty charge/fine can be as much as £80. See Transport for London for full details: www.tfl.gov.uk/tfl/ or call +44 (0) 20 7649 9122.

Car hire

When arranging car hire, you are advised to book and pay before you leave. Prices for hiring a car vary from company to company and depend not only on the size and model of the car but the hire location as well (hiring a car at an airport is likely to be more expensive).

Road toll charges

Motorway tolls

M25, north direction – Dartford Tunnel: £1.00
M25, south direction – Queen Elizabeth II Bridge: £1.00
M48 – Severn Bridge (toll charge for westbound traffic only): £4.60
M4 – Second Severn Crossing (westbound): £4.60
M6 Toll Road – from junction 4 rejoining the M6 at junction 11a: £3.50 during the day, £2.50 at night

Tolls for tunnels and bridges
Tunnel under the Thames (Dartford Tunnel, M25): £1.00
Tunnel under the Mersey (Liverpool): £1.25
Tunnel under the Tyne (Newcastle): £1.00

Queen Elizabeth II Bridge (M25 motorway): £1.00
Severn Bridge (M48 motorway, westbound): £4.60
Second Severn Crossing (M4 motorway, westbound): £4.60
Humber Bridge (A15 road): £2.50
Tamar Bridge (near Plymouth, Devon/Cornwall border A38 road, eastbound): £1.00
Cleddau Bridge (near Pembroke, Dyfed A477 road): £0.75
Forth Bridge (Lothian/Fife A90 road, northbound): £1.00
Tay Bridge (Dundee A914 road, southbound): £0.80
Erskine Bridge (near Glasgow, Strathclyde, A898 road): £0.60
Bridge to the Isle of Skye – Summer: £5.20/Winter: £4.30

Motorcyclists

- On all journeys, the rider and pillion passenger on a motorcycle, scooter or moped must wear a protective helmet.
- Only one pillion passenger can be carried and he/she must sit astride the vehicle on a proper seat and should keep both feet on the footrests.
- Make yourself as visible as possible from the side as well as the front and rear by wearing fluorescent clothing or strips.

BUSES

Throughout the UK buses operate a variety of routes into towns, cities and some villages. The bus routes have been reduced in recent years but it is still a convenient way to get around if you can find a bus timetable in your local area that suits your needs.

Travelling by coach or bus

Most scheduled coach services are run by National Express and Scottish Citylink, allowing you to tour at your own pace on coaches which run to every major town and city in Britain. They are inevitably a little slower than trains but they are an economical alternative. Most coaches are very comfortable and many include refreshments on board. Details about local town and city buses can be obtained from local tourist information centres.

Brit Xplorer

This is a low cost alternative for discovering the UK for overseas (non-British) passport holders. Brit Xplorer allows you to travel on an unlimited amount of journeys operated by National Express within a given period of time, depending on which Brit Xplorer pass you've opted for.

Travel tickets do not need to be booked. All you have to do is show your Brit Xplorer pass to the driver at time of departure. So as long as the coach is not full, you can go on board and travel. Passes and prices: 7-day pass = £79; 14-day pass = £139; a 28-day pass = £219. Visit the website www.nationalexpress.com/save/britxplorer.cfm.

Mega Bus

For low cost inter-city travel, also check out www.megabus.com, which operate discounted bus services between London and 22 major cities within Britain.

London buses

Every weekday over 6,800 scheduled buses carry around six million passengers on over 700 different routes in London, making it one of the largest and most comprehensive urban transport systems in the world.

Comprehensive information can be found on the Transport for London website, www.tfl.gov.uk. There are two cash single fares covering the whole of London. For any bus journey in outer London the fare is just 70p, and for journeys into or from, within, or across central London (Zone 1) the fare is £1.00. If you are 14 or 15, travel is free as soon as you get a Child Oyster photocard. Application forms are available from all Post Offices in London from 1 August 2005. If you are under 14, you can travel free on London's buses and trams from 1 September 2005 without a photocard. Call the Oyster helpline on 0845 330 9876 for more details.

In London there are two types of bus stop which are treated differently:

- White background with red roundel: Compulsory. Buses always stop here unless they are full.
- Red background with white roundel: Request. To stop a bus put out your hand and the bus will stop, unless it is already full. To get off at a Request stop ring the bell once and in good time to let the driver know. Night buses (prefixed with the letter N) treat all stops as Request stops.
- Most of London's buses are red, but some come in other colours; all will display the London Bus Service sign.

London night buses

Nightbirds should note that there's a very good network of night buses (prefixed with the letter 'N') which get you around for a lot less than the price of a taxi. Nearly all of these start at or go via Trafalgar Square. Night buses run all night.

Bus fares

Bus fares can be paid to the driver/conductor once on board the bus. In London it isn't possible to buy a return ticket; therefore a separate ticket will need to be bought for each part of the journey (unless a Travelcard or Oyster card is purchased in advance). For maps of the London bus network, ask at underground stations.

London tour buses

A good introduction to the sights of London is an open-top bus tour. Many companies offer hop-on, hop-off tours with full commentary in English, as well as digitally recorded audio versions in many other languages. Ask your local travel agent or tourist information office for further details.

BLACK CABS AND LICENSED MINICABS

London taxis or black cabs can be hailed in the street if they have a yellow 'For Hire' sign illuminated, or located on designated ranks, which are situated at prominent places, including many mainline rail, underground and bus stations. They are wheelchair accessible and most have a variety of additional aids for disabled customers. The fares charged are regulated, and are clearly shown on a meter in the cab. And with safety paramount, all taxi vehicles and drivers must meet minimum standards (for drivers this includes passing the world renowned 'Knowledge of London' examinations). Licensed vehicles are subject to regular checks by the Public Carriage Office.

Getting a taxi in London

Taxi one-number	0871 871 8710
Computer Cab	020 7432 1432
Dial-A-Cab	020 7253 5000
Radio Taxis	020 7272 0272
Call-A-Cab	020 8901 4444

Xeta	08451 083 000
Zingo ('Hail a taxi by phone')	08700 700 700
DataCab	020 7432 1540

Taxis outside London

Taxis outside London operate in much the same way: the vehicles and drivers are also licensed. Occasionally a traditional taxi can be found but they are more likely to be saloon cars. However, they will still have the illuminated 'For Hire' sign.

Private hire vehicles (minicabs)

The essential difference between taxis and private hire is that private hire journeys must be pre-booked through a licensed operator. Private hire vehicles cannot ply for hire in the street. So you can hire a minicab in person from minicab offices or book by telephoning a local minicab office (telephone numbers can be found in the *Yellow Pages* telephone directory or at www.yell.co.uk. All minicab operators must hold an operating licence issued by the Public Carriage Office. Minicabs do not have a meter so it is advisable to agree a fare before starting your journey. It's inadvisable to accept an offer from drivers touting for business on the street; this is against the law.

LONDON UNDERGROUND (LU)

In 2004/05 LU carried 976 million passengers, an increase of 3 per cent on 2003/4 and the highest figure so far recorded.

London Underground (or the Tube) runs for up to 20 hours a day (times vary according to location), every day and serves all parts of central London; it is one of the easiest ways to travel. Tickets can be purchased from ticket machines and ticket offices at all stations.

Entering and leaving the Underground is made simple by the ticket-operated gates. At the end of your journey, if the value on your ticket is used up, the gate will open but your ticket will be retained. The Underground is divided into six fare zones, with Zone 1 covering central London. Copies of LU maps are available at LU stations and from www.tfl.gov.uk/tfl/.

NATIONAL RAIL

Britain's rail network connects over 2,000 stations with over 18,000 departures everyday. Therefore, there is likely to be a train going your way. The network is modern and efficient and has state-of-the-art trains including the tilting Pendolino train which connects London with cities including Birmingham, Liverpool, Manchester, Glasgow and Edinburgh.

The BritRail range of multi-journey passes and point to point tickets is specially designed to meet the needs of overseas visitors to Britain. These tickets can be used on all of the privatised train companies that operate mainline services in Britain and can be purchased from the shop at www.visitbritain.com or any train station in the UK.

Index of train operating companies (TOCs)

The following train operators operate in the following areas of the UK. You can contact each of the relevant train companies directly or use a centralised telephone and web service. The centralised service allows you to say where you are travelling from and then the relevant train times, train changes, ticket prices for your journey and train operators will be given to you. This service is offered by, among others: http://www.nationalrail.co.uk/, National Rail telephone enquiry line: 0845 748 4950, and www.thetrainline.com/.

Arriva Trains Wales www.arrivatrainswales.co.uk/
c2c www.c2c-online.co.uk/c2c_ticker_index.aspx
Central Trains www.centraltrains.co.uk/
Chiltern Railways www.chilternrailways.co.uk/
Eurostar www.eurostar.com
First Great Western www.firstgreatwestern.co.uk
First Great Western Link www.firstgreatwestern.co.uk
First ScotRail www.firstgroup.com/scotrail/
Gatwick Express www.gatwickexpress.com/
GNER www.gner.co.uk/GNER
Heathrow Connect www.heathrowconnect.com/
Heathrow Express www.heathrowexpress.com/
Hull Trains www.hulltrains.co.uk/
Island Line www.island-line.co.uk/
Merseyrail www.merseyrail.org/
Midland Mainline www.midlandmainline.com/Default.asp?version=7
Northern Rail www.northernrail.org/
one www.onerailway.com/
Silverlink www.silverlink-trains.com/
South Eastern Trains www.setrains.co.uk/setrains
South West Trains http://www.southwesttrains.co.uk/SWTrains
Southern www.southernrailway.com/
Thameslink www.thameslink.co.uk/
TransPennine Express www.tpexpress.co.uk/
Virgin Trains www.virgintrains.co.uk/
WAGN www.wagn.co.uk/
Wessex Trains www.wessextrains.co.uk/

General tips for travelling in the UK

- Smoking is not permitted on the London Underground system or on buses, or trains.

- Keep personal belongings with you at all times to avoid delays caused by security alerts (abandoned luggage may be destroyed).
- Be aware that pickpockets and ticket touts operate in busy areas.
- Travelling outside the 'rush hour' 08:00–09:30 and 17:00–18:00 Monday–Friday is easier and more comfortable.

27

Moving to the UK

SHIPPING/AIR FREIGHT

Once you've decided on the key items you want to take, you'll need to consider how to get it moved to the UK. There are two main options: air or sea.

Shipping

Sea freight costs are worked out by volume so it is the cheapest method of delivery. However, it is also the slowest way to get your belongings to your new home. You should also be aware that Customs and Excise do make random checks which they charge you for – anything from about £25 upwards. All shipping companies should quote for everything except insurance, which you will need to get. You need to nominate the value of the goods and then pay either 3.5 per cent of the value of the goods to cover loss only, or 5 per cent for full insurance. With shipping and insurance you need to shop around. www.intlmovers.com/ is a one-stop shop to source an international moving company that suits your needs. Just enter where you are moving from and to, and up pops a list of companies that can quote for your move. For a list of all worldwide sea freight operators, go to: http://products.kompass.com.

Air freight

Air freight is a much quicker way of getting goods to your new country but is considerably more expensive, with the costs calculated based on weight. So you need to contact airlines and other air freight specialists and get some quotes. The cost may be prohibitive but is worth considering. Post one request and get many offers for both sea and air freight moves from www.OneEntry.com. For a list of all worldwide air freight operators, go to http://products.kompass.com.

Whichever route you choose, make sure you choose a company:

- that is well established and has a proven track record
- that is committed to overseas moving as their core business
- that assumes door-to-door responsibility worldwide
- that is big enough to cope but small enough to care
- that has its own packers and is in the business for the long run.

DECIDING WHAT TO TAKE

How much do you really need? You may find that it will be cheaper to sell some items and buy them new in the UK once you arrive. There are usually lots of friends and family that will take items off your hands if you need them to. Consider the costs of taking all your furniture and bulky items and ask yourself: will they really all fit into your new UK home?

Most people find that moving house, as well as moving country, is a great time to have a good clear-out of all those items you have kept hoarding in the loft, garage, shed, outhouse, etc., for the past few years. Remember, you are moving to a country where you can buy all the things you've ever needed and a whole lot more.

PETS TO THE UK

The Pet Travel Scheme (PETS) allows cats and dogs to enter the UK without the period of quarantine that was previously required.

To travel to the UK under the PETS scheme, the pet must:

1. be fitted with a microchip
2. be vaccinated against rabies
3. be blood tested to show a satisfactory level of protection against rabies
4. be treated against ticks and a type of tapeworm
5. have a declaration of residency completed by the owner
6. be issued with an official PETS certificate
7. be issued with an Animal Welfare Export certificate.

The whole process will take a minimum of about seven months, as the blood test for the level of rabies protection must be taken at least six months prior to entry into the UK.

It is worth noting that certain breeds of dogs such as Pit Bull Terriers, Japanese Tosas, Dogo Argentinos and Fila Brasilieros, or any animal which appears to have been bred for fighting, will not be allowed entry.

For further information visit www.defra.gov.uk/animalh/animindx.htm for an introduction to animal health and welfare from the UK government and more details about the PETS scheme.

BEFORE YOU DEPART FOR THE UK

Here are just a few things we suggest you organise before your departure:

- Arrange appointments for relevant inoculations.
- Arrange travel/medical insurance.
- Notify doctor and obtain medical history/records, details of medication where necessary.
- Obtain eye prescription from optician.

- Request dental records from dentist.
- Transfer or set up new UK bank accounts.
- Cancel store cards.
- Notify credit card companies.
- Advise tax department you are leaving the county and get advice.
- Cancel service providers – electricity, gas, water, council tax, telecoms providers, TV licence, etc.
- Redirect mail through the post office.
- Send out change of address cards.
- Clear out unwanted belongings.
- Put items you are not taking into storage.
- Make a list of everything you are going to take.
- Use up food from freezer.
- Organise disconnection of domestic appliances.
- Cancel any regular deliveries (milk, newspapers).
- Take down curtains and blinds.
- Pay all outstanding bills.
- Make sure you have your driver's licence, car registration and insurance records.
- Make arrangements for moving your pets and any house plants; they cannot usually be taken in the movers' van.

On the day

- Pack small valuables separately.
- Pack essential items in your hand luggage.
- Confirm service meter readings and keep a spare copy of readings.
- Switch off power and water supplies (if necessary).
- Lock all windows and doors.
- Deposit keys with estate or rental agent.

28

Arriving in the UK

You've finally arrived! If you've travelled by air, you will probably arrive at one of the main international airports in London – Heathrow or Gatwick or one of the big regional airports – Manchester or Glasgow. If you have arrived by sea you will probably arrive at one of the Channel Ports — Dover, Folkestone or Harwich are the most likely.

Once you've collected your baggage and passed through Customs, you will need to start your onward journey to your final destination and your new home. If you need to use trains, coaches or taxis, try to book them in advance so you can relax a little once you land. Likewise, if you are planning to stay a night before moving on, it would be best to book a hotel room in advance before you arrive in the UK.

LINKS FROM THE MAIN AIRPORTS

Heathrow. Heathrow is one of the world's busiest airports. There are coach connections, a Tube station (on the Piccadilly line, marked in dark blue on the Tube map) and the 'Heathrow Express' train service to Paddington station in London.

Gatwick. There are coach connections, and a train service from Gatwick to central London (Victoria or Kings Cross stations, depending on which train you catch). There is also a 'Gatwick Express' train service direct to London's Victoria station.

Stansted. There are local connections and coach services and a 'Stansted Express' train service to Liverpool Street station in London.

Luton. There is a coach service and train service (via shuttle bus from the airport) to central London.

Using the London Underground (Tube)

All tube stations feature on the famous London Underground map. This details the different Tube lines in different colours and allows you to see at which stations you can transfer from one line to another. If you are planning to use the Tube, remember that you may have to change trains to get to your destination. At some stations this can be difficult if you have a lot of luggage. The Tube can be extremely crowded at 'rush hour' on weekdays (Monday to Friday).

MONEY FOR YOUR IMMEDIATE NEEDS

When you arrive in the UK, you should have about £250 in cash and travellers' cheques for your immediate needs (meals, train fares, etc.). Avoid carrying any more cash in case it gets lost or stolen. Most shops and hotels will accept credit cards, and some will also accept payment by sterling travellers' cheques.

The vast majority of shops and services in the UK will accept payment in UK currency only. You may also be able to withdraw money from ATM ('cash') machines as long as you have a Personal Identification Number (PIN) for that card.

PUBLIC PHONE BOXES

In case your mobile phone isn't working, you will find public telephones at all airports, sea ports, railway stations, bus stations and on many streets. They accept coins from 20 pence upwards and most phone boxes also accept phone cards as well as coins. These can be purchased from most convenience shops and newsagents.

USEFUL CONTACTS

Traveline

www.traveline.org.uk Tel: +44 870 608 2 608 (from outside UK) 0870 608 2 608 (from inside UK) – lines usually open 8am to 8pm. Information on transport services throughout the UK. Website includes a travel planner facility.

National Rail Enquiries

www.nationalrail.co.uk Tel: 0044 20 7278 5240 (from outside UK) 08457 484950 (from within UK)
Information on all UK rail services.

Airport express train services

Heathrow Express: www.heathrowexpress.com Tel: 0845 600 1515
Gatwick Express: www.gatwickexpress.co.uk Tel: 0845 850 1530
Stansted Express www.stanstedexpress.co.uk Tel: 0845 8500 150

National Express coach services

www.nationalexpress.com Tel: 08705 80 80 80

Scottish Citylink coach services

www.citylink.co.uk Tel: 08705 50 50 50

Transport for London

www.tfl.gov.uk Tel: 020 7222 1234 (24 hours)
Covers bus, tube, train and other services in London.

The British Airport Authority

www.baa.co.uk Information about Heathrow, Gatwick, Stansted, Glasgow, Edinburgh, Aberdeen and Southampton airports.

29

Lifestyle and leisure

The UK has a full range of activities available. Therefore the lifestyle, although heavily work focused, still allows a 'community' atmosphere in most villages and towns and even in some cities. Most people are fairly relaxed but the British are a very proud people when it comes to national sports like football, rugby and cricket.

Depending on where you live or where you visit, you are never far away from the sea. To give you an idea of Britain's size, here are some facts and figures for you:

- With an area of about 242,000 sq km (93,000 sq miles), Britain is just under 1,000 km (about 600 miles) from the south coast to the extreme north of Scotland and just under 500 km (around 300 miles) across at the widest point.
- The coastline of Great Britain is 14,549 km (9,040 miles) with England and Wales, including islands, taking up 5,214 km (8,389 miles) of this figure and Scotland, including islands, 9,335 km (5,800 miles).
- The most northerly point on the British mainland is Dunnet Head, north-east Scotland, and the most southerly, Lizard Point, Cornwall.
- From areas of flat land, 2,000 miles of navigable canals and several mountain ranges, the landscape is varied.

LEISURE ACTIVITIES

Pubs

You will find that pubs play a large part in British culture and are the most popular places to socialise in. In London, Leicester Square, Soho, Old Street and Charing Cross Road are probably the most central and popular areas for going out.

In terms of the regulations, you have to be over 18 years old to drink, buy or attempt to buy alcohol. It is also an offence for any person under the age of 18 to buy or attempt to buy alcoholic liquor or to consume alcohol on licensed premises, although there are some exceptions.

The new licensing law has allowed many of Britain's 113,000 pubs, clubs and bars to apply for new longer opening licences, giving them flexible opening hours, with the potential to open 24 hours a day, seven days a week. The new law came into effect in November 2005, although it is unlikely that pubs will stay open around the clock.

Cinemas and video/DVD hire

Cinemas are a good option on a cold or grey evening. The largest cinema in London is the Odeon (0870 5050 007 – www.odeon.co.uk) in Leicester Square, while the Empire, across the square, is another popular cinema. UGC is also one of the major cinema chains in the UK, as is Vue. Expect to pay around £6.50 for an adult ticket. All films receive a UK classification before they are released. The categories are: U = universal suitable for anyone aged four or over; PG = parental guidance suitable for general viewing but some scenes may not be suitable for children without guidance from parents; 12 = no one under 12 admitted unless with an adult; 15 = no one under 15 permitted; 18 = no one under 18 permitted. Video and DVD hire shops are located across the UK. One of the largest is Blockbuster. The classification of each film is shown on the cover.

Sports

The main sports the British are passionate about and take part in are: rugby, football, cricket, golf, tennis, Formula One and athletics. Obviously with London hosting the 2012 Olympics, it is hoped that many more people use sport as a leisure pursuit.

Eating out

Whether it's a pub lunch or a gourmet dinner, there are lots of restaurants across the UK serving some of the best food in the world.

Theatres

London's West End is most famous for its large-scale productions. The Royal National Theatre and the Barbican Theatre host a wide variety of quality dramas. For dance, opera and music, the London Coliseum, Sadlers Wells and Royal Opera House are at the forefront. Regional theatres across the UK also features top West End productions on tour and are a really good evening out. Listings of shows are available in national and London newspapers and magazines such as *Time Out*. For discounted tickets for West End shows and for booking tickets on the day of the performance, either go direct to the theatre for standby tickets or returns (ring ahead for availability) or, for genuine discount tickets, buy in person from the **tkts** booth in the clocktower building on the south side of London's Leicester Square and at Canary Wharf Docklands Light Railway Station.

Useful websites

www.pubsulike.co.uk/
www.londontown.com/
www.londinium.com/
www.touchlondon.co.uk/
www.london-eating.co.uk/
www.fancyapint.com/
www.ugccinemas.co.uk
www.myvue.com/
www.gumtree.com/
www.londonolympics2012.com/
home.skysports.com/
www.rfu.com/
www.thefa.com/
www.icc-cricket.com/
www.toptable.co.uk/
www.londontheatre.co.uk/
www.officiallondontheatre.co.uk/tkts

WHERE TO GO AND WHAT TO DO

Wherever you are going to be based in the UK, famous historical and picturesque places are never far away.

NB: All times are approximate

From London to:	Driving (miles)	Air	Train	Coach
Bath	106	n/a	1hr 30mins	2hr 25mins
Belfast	340	1hr 25mins	10hr 35mins	11hr
Birmingham	114	n/a	1hr 45mins	2hr 40mins
Brighton	51	n/a	51mins	1hr 45mins
Cambridge	56	n/a	50mins	1hr 50mins
Canterbury	62	n/a	1hr 35mins	1hr 45mins
Cardiff	145	n/a	2hr 05mins	3hr 5mins
Chester	179	n/a	2hr 40mins	5hr 30mins
Durham	255	n/a	3hr	6hr

From London to:	Driving (miles)	Air	Train	Coach
Edinburgh	393	1hr 30mins	4hr 30mins	8hr 45mins
Exeter	174	n/a	2hr 30mins	4hr 15mins
Glasgow	402	1hr 30mins	5hr 30mins	7hr 55mins
Inverness	568	1hr 45mins	8hr 10mins	12hr 26mins
Jersey	220	1hr	6hr 55mins	7hr 55mins
Liverpool	193	n/a	3hr	4hr 30mins
Manchester	184	1hr	2hr 40mins	4hr 15mins
Newcastle-upon-Tyne	270	1hr 10mins	3hr	6hr 25mins
Norwich	115	n/a	1hr 50mins	2hr 40mins
Oxford	64	n/a	1hr 05mins	1hr 30mins
Portsmouth	70	n/a	1hr 40mins	2hr 15mins
Salisbury	84	n/a	1hr 30mins	2hr 40mins
Southampton	80	n/a	1hr 20mins	2hr
Stratford-upon-Avon	121	n/a	2hr 12mins	2hr 45mins
Windermere	259	n/a	4hr 10mins	6hr 55mins
York	188	n/a	2hr	4hr 15mins

TOP TOURIST ATTRACTIONS IN LONDON

1. Tate Modern, Sumner Street, SE1 (020) 7887 8000 www.tate.org.uk
2. The London Eye, Jubilee Gardens, SE1 (0870) 500 0600 www.londoneye.com
3. The Tower of London, Tower Hill, EC3 (020) 7709 0765 www.hrp.org.uk
4. HMS *Belfast*, Morgan's Lane, Tooley Street, SE1 (020) 7940 6328 ww.hmsbelfast.co.uk
5. London Zoo, Regent's Park, NW1 (020) 7722 3333 www.londonzoo.co.uk
6. Madame Tussaud's, Marylebone Road, NW1 (020) 7935 6861 www.madame-tussauds.com/
7. British Museum, Great Russell Street, WC1 (020) 7636 1555 www.thebritishmuseum.ac.uk
8. Freemasons' Hall Great Queen Street, WC2 (020) 7831 9811
9. Houses of Parliament, Parliament Square, SW1 (020) 7219 4272 www.parliament.uk

10. Highgate Cemetery, Swain's Lane, N6 (020) 8340 1834 http://highgate-cemetery.org
11. Houses of Parliament and Big Ben
12. Buckingham Palace – home of the Queen
13. Leicester Square – the heart of the West End and theatreland
14. St Paul's Cathedral – the famous cathedral designed by Sir Christopher Wren
15. Tower Bridge – one of London's best known landmarks
16. London Planetarium – where you can look to the sky
17. Oxford Street – Europe's longest shopping street
18. Piccadilly Circus – home of the famous Eros statue and giant illuminated billboard
19. Regent Street – famous shops include Hamleys toy store and Liberty department store
20. Westminster Abbey – the venue for coronations.

OTHER TOP UK ATTRACTIONS

Alton Towers, Staffordshire www.altontowers.com/resort/

Legoland, Windsor www.lego.com/legoland/windsor/

Windsor Castle, Berkshire www.windsor.gov.uk/attractions/castle.htm

Edinburgh Castle, Edinburgh www.historic-scotland.gov.uk/

Chester Zoo, Cheshire www.chesterzoo.org/

The Eden Project, Cornwall www.edenproject.com/

Kew Gardens, London www.rbgkew.org.uk/welcome.html

Roman Baths and Pump Room, Bath www.romanbaths.co.uk/

Blackpool Pleasure Beach, Lancashire www.blackpoolpleasurebeach.com/

York Minster Yorkshire www.yorkminster.org/

EUROSTAR AND EUROTUNNEL

Why not pop to Paris for lunch! With France so close, the Eurostar and Eurotunnel offer a quick and relaxing way to be in the centre of Paris in less than three hours!

- Eurostar – a direct link between Paris, Lille, Brussels and London (Waterloo), Ashford (Kent) on Eurostar trains. This service is for foot passengers only and runs every hour (between 05:00 and 20:00) and takes approximately 3 hours. Contact: 08705 186186
- Eurotunnel – carries passengers and their vehicles and operates between Calais and Folkestone. Trains run 24 hours. Between 06:00 and midnight there are three trains an hour, between midnight and 06:00 a service operates every two hours. Contact: 08705 353535.

NEED MORE IDEAS ON THINGS TO DO?

www.english-heritage.org.uk/
www.visitwales.com/
www.visitbritain.com/vb3-en-gb/default.aspx
www.nationaltrust.org.uk/main/
www.timeout.com/london/
www.hrp.org.uk/webcode/home.asp

30

Useful information – things you need to know

CURRENCY IN THE UK

The UK has a decimal-based currency known as sterling, or more commonly known as pounds. 100 pence equals £1 (one pound sterling).

A variety of coinage and notes are available as are detailed below. The UK has not converted to the euro. However, when travelling to many of the other main European countries, e.g., France, Spain, Italy, Greece, you should be aware that they all use the single euro currency.

UK Coins

1 penny = 1p (smallest copper-coloured coin)
2 pence = 2p (copper coloured)
5 pence = 5p (smallest silver coin)
10 pence = 10p (silver coin)
20 pence = 20p (silver coin)
50 pence = 50p (largest silver coin)
£1 = 100 p (gold coloured)
£2 = 200p (largest gold coloured)

UK notes

£5 = 500p Blue/green
£10 = 1000p Brown
£20 = 2000p Purple
£50 = 5000p Red/orange

TIPPING

Tipping in the UK is not always appropriate. If you feel you received good service and you want to show your appreciation, here is a guide to customary practice.

- Hotels
  Most hotel bills include a service charge, usually 10–12 per cent. Where a service charge is not included in a hotel restaurant, it is customary to give 10–15 per cent of the restaurant bill and for rooms an optional amount to room staff.

- Restaurants
  Some restaurant bills include a service charge. Where a service charge is not included it is customary to leave a tip of 10–15 per cent of the bill. Some restaurants now include a suggested tip in the bill total.

- Taxis
  10–15 per cent of the fare

- Porterage
  Discretionary

- Hairdressers
  Discretionary

COST OF LIVING

London is one of the world's most expensive cities. The semi-annual cost-of-living survey by the Economist Intelligence Unit puts London ninth on the world list. Across the world, living in a capital city is more expensive than living in the provinces. In the UK, living in Manchester, for example, is 16 per cent cheaper than in London.

As with most comparisons, the cost of living in the UK really does depend on each individual's situation. However, often a person staying in the UK for a few years can effectively minimise major expenses by renting a car, sharing a house and using public transport wherever possible.

But one thing you shouldn't do is keep converting the cost of an item from UK pounds into your previous currency. It can seriously distort your view and enjoyment of UK life.

The following are some rough examples of what it can cost to live in the UK.

Average UK cost of food and drink	
Weekly grocery bill	£60
Pub meal	£6
Restaurant meal	£18
Pint of beer	£2.50–£3
Bottle of wine	£8
Meal for two in mid-priced restaurant	£40

UK cost of transportation	
Weekly Zone 1–6 London Travelcard	£30
Monthly Zone 1–2 London Travelcard	£70
Train trip London to Edinburgh	£92
Train trip to Cambridge/Brighton	£20
Avg mid-sized car rental for a weekend	£70
Return budget flight to Spain	£150
Eurostar return ticket to Paris	£110
Return flight to Ireland	£100

UK cost of entertainment	
Movie	£7–£10
West End play	£25

OPENING A BANK ACCOUNT

Ideally you should open a UK-based bank account at least five weeks before you leave for the UK. Your existing bank at home should be able to organise this for you through affiliations they have with UK banks. Then all you have to do is arrange to collect your cheque book and debit card from your new local branch when you arrive in the UK.

If you can't or haven't made arrangements before you leave, you can expect opening a UK bank account to take two weeks or more and to be a tedious process of form filling and identification. Most Banks request you to open a bank account in person. The type of items that they require you to take as proof of identity varies, but could include at least two of the following items:

- passport
- national identity card
- residence permit
- national driving licence
- tenancy agreement for your new home in the UK
- a letter from your employer in the UK confirming your address, salary, etc.
- proof of your previous or permanent address in the country you came from
- a letter from your previous bank or your agreement that they may contact them.

This list is not exhaustive. However, the best approach if you are going into a UK bank to open an account is to take as many original documents with you as possible. Banks will not accept copies so remember to take originals.

BANKS AND BUILDING SOCIETIES

There are lots of well known high-street banks and building societies in the UK. The following is a list of some of the most common ones you will see on most high streets.

Abbey	Co-operative Bank
Alliance and Leicester	Halifax
Bank of Scotland	HSBC
Barclays Bank	Lloyds TSB
Bradford & Bingley	Nat West
Bristol and West	Royal Bank of Scotland
Britannia Building Society	Yorkshire Bank
Cheltenham & Gloucester	Woolwich
Clydesdale Bank	

Most banks and building societies require you to operate your bank account for a period until they will provide/offer you with additional services. This gives them a chance to see your salary being paid in and your bills being paid out. They will also check that you will be using your debit card for cash withdrawals and payments responsibly. Depending on which bank you open your account with, the time will vary on how long before you can ask for an overdraft facility, a more complex bank account or a credit card.

Building societies

These are different from banks. Building societies are traditionally known more for savings accounts and mortgage lending; however, in recent years a number have been bought out by banks and have also diversified their services to include current accounts, cash machines, credit cards, foreign exchange desks, insurance and loans.

Online banks

All the major UK banks offer Internet banking services so you can manage your account remotely, from wherever you are. However, there are also a number of banks that just operate an online service and consequently do not have a high street presence. These include: Egg; Smile and One account, among others. They are usually all subsidiaries of the leading financial banking providers listed above but operate as separate businesses. Opening an account with one of these Internet banks still requires proof of identity, but as they have no high-street presence, proof (originals only) has to be sent by post. You will then have to wait until they have conducted their checks before your account is open and fully functional. Documents will then be returned to you by post.

Further information

The British Bankers' Association represents all the UK's financial services firms and also provides help on how to open a bank account. They can be contacted at www.bba.org.uk.

POSTAGE SYSTEM

Sending mail within Britain

Royal Mail is the official mail service in Britain. They provide two main services:

- First Class - aims to deliver all First Class letters and packages by the next working day.

- Second Class – aims to deliver all Second Class letters and packages within 3 working days.

Please note that all postal charges are based on weight.

Weight (in grams) up to:	First Class	Second Class
60g	32p	23p
100g	49p	37p
150g	68p	50p
200g	84p	62p
250g	99p	75p
300g	£1.14	88p
350g	£1.29	1.00
400g	£1.49	£1.21
450g	£1.70	£1.39
500g	£1.90	£1.55
600g	£2.30	£1.78
700g	£2.69	£2.01
750g	£2.89	£2.12
800g	£3.10	
900g	£3.49	
1kg	£3.89	
Items over 1kg	Plus 85p for each 250g or part thereof	

The Royal Mail also offers 'Special Delivery' and 'Recorded' services as well as international airmail services to all locations across the world.

There are a number of private courier services, which are listed in the *Yellow Pages* and at www.yell.co.uk, which you can use for UK or international deliveries.

For further information about sending mail within Britain, phone Royal Mail Customer Services on +44 (0)8457 740 740 or visit www.royalmail.com.

Sending mail from Britain

There are two options for sending mail abroad weighing up to 2kg: airmail and surface mail. Airmail is simple and quick, whereas surface mail is cheaper but takes longer.

Airmail postage for postcards and letters up to 20g is 44p to Europe; anywhere else in the world for 72p.

All postal packets (excluding letters) to destinations outside the European Union are liable to examination by Customs authorities. It is important you check whether you need to fill in a Customs declaration before you post your package.

A detailed price list for airmail and surface mail is available from Post Offices or via the Royal Mail/Post Office website www.royal mail.com.

Postage stamps

Postage stamps may be bought from a variety of outlets, including newsagents, post offices, petrol stations and card shops. They are sold in books of six or 12 first- or second-class stamps.

Post office opening hours

Post offices are generally open from 09:00–17:30, Monday to Friday.

Main post offices are also open 09:00–12:30 on Saturday. Please note that exact opening hours vary depending on the size and location of the branch. For information on individual post offices' opening times, call Post Office Enquiries on +44 (0)8457 223344.

VOTING – WHO CAN VOTE?

To vote in parliamentary elections in the UK you must be a British citizen, a citizen of another Commonwealth country or of the Irish Republic, as well as being resident in the UK, aged 18 or over, included in the register of electors for the constituency and not subject to any legal incapacity to vote. Visit www.electoralcommission.org.uk.

People not entitled to vote include members of the House of Lords, foreign nationals resident in the UK (other than Commonwealth citizens or citizens of the Irish Republic), some patients detained under mental health legislation, sentenced prisoners and people convicted within the previous five years of corrupt or illegal election practices.

To vote in your own country

Most countries will allow you to vote in elections back in your own country, provided you intend to return home at some point. Typically postal voting is the easiest to do, although your country's embassy may also have voting booths in their buildings located in the UK. To vote in your own country you do need to check you are on the electoral roll. If you aren't, you will need to speak to your embassy. Your country's government websites will carry details of voting procedures while you are abroad. Some of the main country sites are:

www.elections.org.nz (NZ)
www.aec.gov.au (Australia)
www.elections.org.sa (South Africa)
www.elections.ca (Canada)

MEDIA

Every aspect of business and all sectors of industry and the services are represented and reported in the national press and media, including print, television, radio and online content. Printed media are by far the biggest source of information. The main national newspaper for UK business audiences is the *Financial Times* (FT). This covers finance and investment, stock exchanges and commodity markets, employment and recruitment, mergers and acquisitions, market analysis and comment, industry sectors, marketing, personnel and international developments. Through FT.com there is also substantial online information, including a global archive of reports and news items covering the international business spectrum.

Other national newspapers provide daily business news coverage and each industry sector and sub-sector has at least one trade publication providing detailed coverage of specialised service and manufacturing industries in the UK. Nationwide media directories such as Pimms and Benns provide details of what is available in each trade sector. Printed and online information about local and regional markets is also available through Chambers of Commerce. Central government departments, such as the Department of Trade and Industry, and local government authorities provide regularly updated literature and online information for the business community. The BBC online service provides market and business information which is updated throughout each day.

UK media facts and figures

- Over **53** per cent of UK households have access to digital television. (Source:Ofcom end of March 2004).

- As of 12 June 2004, there were 3 national radio licences, **276** local radio licences, **1** national digital multiplex licence, **44** local digital multiplex licences, over **4,600** short-term restricted service licences, **120** Radio Licensable Content Service Licences, **122** long-term restricted service licences, **1** analogue additional service licence, **68** Local and **11** National Digital Service Programme Licences, and **19** Digital Additional Service Licences.

Useful sites

www.bbc.co.uk – 24hr news from the BBC with links to all the BBC's local radio stations across the UK

www.ft.com – the *Financial Times* online

www.ftse.com – in-depth information from the world-renowned index calculation specialist

www.insider.co.uk – Scotland's national business magazine. News, information and features for regional markets

www.economist.com – the UK's premier online and offline source for economics and business news and analysis

www.sky.com – latest satellite news from around the world and much more

www.newspapersoc.org.uk – details most newspaper titles in Britain

www.radio-now.co.uk – links to websites of all radio stations throughout Britain

www.itc.org.uk – details of all television stations throughout the UK.

www.mediauk.com – directory of television and radio stations, and newspapers throughout the UK

INTERNET AND TELEPHONES

Internet cafes are everywhere in the UK and you can connect for as little as 50p for half an hour.

If you can get connected at home, some of the major Internet providers such as AOL are always running free trials for up to two months before you choose whether to sign up with them. With such competition in the market from Tiscali, Freeserve, AOL, BT, Orange, etc., the monthly cost of connection continues to reduce. Broadband is widely available.

Landlines

British Telecom is the main telephone provider of landlines. They will connect you within a day and charge you a quarterly standing charge for the connection.

Mobiles

Thanks to healthy competition it can often be cheaper to use a mobile telephone than have a landline connected. Shop around as most providers offer free talk minutes and texting bundles if you sign up for a 12-month contract.

Pay-as-you-go mobiles

The beauty of pay-as-you-go is that you don't incur line rental or surcharges and you just pay for the time you use it. You pre-pay using top-up cards available from shops, newsagents, petrol stations, supermarkets and follow the instructions on the top-up card to register your phone credit. You will need to pay for a handset, which could be £100 plus, or you may be able to use your original mobile phone and just buy a UK pre-pay SIM card for £10 to put into it.

Payphones

Located on streets and in airports, train stations and other major public venues, public payphones will accept cash and credit card payments. Using cash, the minimum fee for making a domestic call is 30p (which includes 10p connection charge). Local and national calls are charged at 30p for the first 15 minutes, then 10p for each seven minutes and 30 seconds thereafter. Using credit or debit cards the minimum fee for local and national calls is 95p (which includes 75p connection charge).

The minimum fee for international calls, calls to premium rate numbers, calls to mobile phones or calls made via the operator is £1.20p (which includes a £1 connection charge).

VOLTAGE

The standard electrical voltage in Britain is 240 V AC, 50Hz. A three-square pronged adapter plug and/or electric converter for appliances is required.

PETS

Strict laws apply in the UK which require owners to care for their animals and make sure they do not suffer unnecessarily. The RSPCA employs many inspectors to prosecute owners and also care for abandoned animals.

All dogs in public places must wear a collar, showing the name and address of the owner and must be kept under control. Dog owners should ensure their dogs do not foul footpaths.

REFUSE COLLECTION

Every home in Britain has a regular waste collection service. It is provided by the local council and will almost always be made on the same day, or days, each week. Contact your local council for details of which day applies to your local address. To find your local council services, go to www.direct.gov.uk, look in your local telephone directory, or look on www.yell.com.

LANGUAGE

English is the official language in the UK. Regional dialects exist and some of the traditional languages of Gaelic and Welsh are still spoken in some areas. If English is not your first language, it can be tiring listening and interpreting conversations every day and even if you are a fluent English speaker it is possible that some regional accents make it harder for you to understand what is being said. In certain areas of the UK you may find people speak quickly and you may feel embarrassed to ask them to repeat what they have said. However, in most cases, people will slow down or speak more clearly if you ask.

RELIGION

- Christianity is the main religion in Great Britain. There were 41 million Christians in 2001, making up almost three-quarters of the population (72 per cent). This group included the Church of England, Church of Scotland, Church in Wales, Catholic, Protestant and all other Christian denominations.

- People with no religion formed the second largest group, comprising 15 per cent of the population.

- About one in 20 (5 per cent) of the population belonged to a non-Christian religious denomination.

- Muslims were the largest religious group after Christians. There were 1.6 million Muslims living in Britain in 2001. This group comprised 3 per cent of the total population and over half (52 per cent) of the non-Christian religious population.

- Hindus were the second largest non-Christian religious group. There were over half a million Hindus (558,000), comprising 1 per cent of the total population and 18 per cent of the non-Christian religious population.
- There were just over a third of a million Sikhs (336,000), making up 0.6 per cent of the total population and 11 per cent of the non-Christian religious population.
- There were just over a quarter of a million Jewish people (267,000), constituting 0.5 per cent of the total population and 9 per cent of the non-Christian religious group.
- Buddhists numbered 149,000 people in 2001, comprising 0.3 per cent of the population of Great Britain.

Geographical religious breakdown

Based on the UK government's 2001 population census:

- People from non-Christian religions are more likely to live in England than in Scotland or Wales. In 2001 they made up 6 per cent of the population in England, compared with only 2 per cent in Wales and 1 per cent in Scotland.
- People from Jewish, Hindu, Buddhist, Muslim and Sikh backgrounds were concentrated in London and other large urban areas. Christians and those with no religion were more evenly dispersed across the country.

UTILITIES

There are an increasing number of companies offering utility services such as gas and electricity. Some of the more popular or useful sites and contact details are listed below.

Gas and electric

www.uswitch.com – compare gas and electric prices and switch suppliers

www.house.co.uk – British Gas

www.theenergypeople.com – services from Scottish Power

Water and sewerage

www.ofwat.gov.uk/aptrix/ofwat/publish.nsf/Content/watercompanyaddresstelephone – the UK regulator provides a full list of all the UK water and sewerage companies with their contact details.

Council tax

www.direct.gov.uk – provides the latest information on UK public services

www.voa.gov.uk/ – details the council tax bands for all UK properties.

BRITISH SUMMER TIME

Every spring we change time in the UK to recognise British Summer Time when the clocks go forward one hour. Clocks go back one hour in the autumn to Greenwich Mean Time.

BANK AND PUBLIC HOLIDAYS IN ENGLAND, WALES AND NORTHERN IRELAND

The expected dates of bank and public holidays in England, Wales and Northern Ireland for the years 2006–2008 inclusive are listed below. Dates for Scotland are determined by the Scottish Executive.

	2006	2007	2008
England and Wales			
New Year's Day	2 Jan*	1 Jan	1 Jan
Good Friday	14 Apr	6 Apr	21 Mar
Easter Monday	17 Apr	9 Apr	24 Mar
Early May Bank Holiday	1 May	7 May	5 May
Spring Bank Holiday	29 May	28 May	26 May
Summer Bank Holiday	28 Aug	27 Aug	25 Aug
Christmas Day	25 Dec	25 Dec	25 Dec
Boxing Day	26 Dec	26 Dec	26 Dec
* Substitute Bank Holiday in lieu of 1 Jan			
Northern Ireland (NI)			
New Year's Day	2 Jan*	1 Jan	1 Jan
St Patrick's Day	17 Mar	19 Mar	17 Mar
Good Friday	14 Apr	6 Apr	21 Mar
Easter Monday	17 Apr	9 Apr	24 Mar
Early May Bank Holiday	1 May	7 May	5 May
Spring Bank Holiday	29 May	28 May	26 May
Battle of the Boyne (Orangemen's Day)	12 July	12 July	14 July
Summer Bank Holiday	28 Aug	27 Aug	25 Aug
Christmas Day	25 Dec	25 Dec	25 Dec
Boxing Day	26 Dec	26 Dec	26 Dec
*Substitute Bank Holiday in lieu of 1 Jan			

UK National Saint Day Holidays

1 March	St David's Day, national day of Wales
17 March	St Patrick's Day, national day of Northern Ireland and Republic of Ireland
23 April	St George's Day, national day of England
30 November	St Andrew's Day, national day of Scotland

WEATHER AND CLIMATE

Whatever the season, the British weather is liable to change from day to day, so if you're wondering what to pack, a good idea is to bring layers, a waterproof coat or jacket and an umbrella.

Autumn (September–November)

In autumn there can be very warm days, but equally there can be very cold ones too. Temperatures fluctuate around 7 to 14 degrees Celsius but are likely to be much warmer in September than November.

Winter (December–early March)

Winter sees Britain's shortest and coldest days (about 7–8 hours of daylight) but these can be crisp and bright. Temperatures fluctuate from around 1 to 5 degrees Celsius.

Spring (March–May)

In spring, you might enjoy wonderful sunny weather but then, it might equally be cold and wet. Temperatures fluctuate from around 6 to 11 degrees Celsius. May has warm days – up to about 18 degrees Celsius.

Summer (June–August)

Most days in summer are warm, but evenings can be cool. Temperatures average around 14–20 degrees Celsius, although it can be up to around 28 degrees Celsius on some days.

There is quite a difference in temperature between Scotland and southern England. Generally, the further north, the colder it is likely to be.

Europe's climate is as variable as everything else about the Continent. In northwestern Europe – Benelux, Denmark, south-western Norway, most of France and parts of Germany, as well as the British Isles – the climate is basically a cool temperate one, with the chance of rain all year round and no great extremes of either cold or hot weather.

There is no bad time to travel in most of this part of the Continent, although the winter months between November and March can be damp and miserable – especially in the upland regions – and obviously the summer period between May and September sees the most reliable and driest weather.

(Temperatures are quoted in Celsius and Fahrenheit)

	Jan	Feb	March	April	May	June	July	Aug	Sept	Oct	Nov	Dec
Amsterdam	4/40	5/42	9/49	13/56	18/64	21/70	22/72	22/71	19/67	14/57	9/48	6/42
Brussels	4/40	7/42	10/51	14/58	18/65	22/72	23/73	22/72	21/69	15/60	9/48	6/42
Dublin	8/46	8/47	10/50	13/55	15/60	18/65	20/67	19/67	17/63	14/57	10/51	8/47
Lisbon	14/57	15/59	17/63	20/67	21/71	25/77	27/81	28/82	26/79	22/72	17/63	15/58
London	**6/43**	**7/44**	**10/50**	**13/56**	**17/62**	**20/69**	**22/71**	**22/71**	**19/65**	**14/58**	**10/50**	**7/45**
Madrid	9/47	11/52	15/59	18/65	21/70	27/80	31/87	30/85	25/77	19/65	13/55	9/48
Paris	6/43	7/45	12/54	16/60	20/68	23/73	25/76	24/75	21/70	16/60	10/50	7/44
Rome	11/52	13/55	15/59	19/66	23/74	28/82	30/87	30/86	26/79	22/71	16/61	13/55

WHAT TO WEAR IN THE UK

If you come from a warm climate, you may find it uncomfortable to wear heavy winter clothing.

FITNESS

It is part of everyday culture in the UK to go to the gym or take some form of exercise. However, many people fail to stick with their good intentions. A number of major employers across the UK have gyms and other sports facilities onsite to help encourage their employees to have a healthy mind and body.

There are a number of major health club chains in the UK. Here are just a selection. Check to see what special introductory offers they may have.

www.lafitness.co.uk
www.davidlloydleisure.co.uk
www.holmesplace.com
www.cannons.co.uk

31

Crossing the cultural divide

The UK is made up of three different countries and a province: England, Scotland, Wales and the province of Northern Ireland. These countries all have very different characters and identities. The United Kingdom is a diverse and multi-ethnic society, where people of all backgrounds are welcome and their involvement in local communities is valued.

The UK has a long tradition of welcoming migrants and refugees from around the world, many of whom have settled permanently.

All major world religions are represented – Mosques, Sikh temples, synagogues and Buddhist and Hindu places of worship can be seen alongside a whole range of Christian churches, from Anglican and Roman Catholic through to Nonconformist and Orthodox.

Many languages are represented. The most widely spoken South Asian language in the UK is Punjabi, followed by Urdu, Bengali and Gujarati. The main Chinese dialects spoken in the UK are Cantonese and Mandarin.

All this diversity means that, when you come to the UK, you will find it easy to settle in. You will also develop an enhanced understanding of different cultures by meeting others from an enormous variety of religious and national backgrounds.

WHAT IS CULTURE SHOCK? (from www.ukcosa.org.uk)

'Culture shock' describes the impact of moving from a familiar culture to one which is unfamiliar. It is an experience described by people who have travelled abroad to work, live or study. It can affect anyone and includes the shock of a new environment, meeting lots of new people and learning the ways of a different country. It also includes the shock of being separated from the important people in your life. Our cycle of emotions when moving to a new country can be a real rollercoaster ride! The following factors contribute to culture shock:

Food

You may find British food strange. It may taste different, or be cooked differently, or it may seem bland or heavy. So try to find a supplier of familiar food, and eat plenty of fresh fruit and vegetables.

Social roles

Social behaviours may confuse, surprise or offend you. For example, you may find people appear cold and distant or always in a hurry. This may be particularly likely in the centre of large cities.

'Rules' of behaviour

As well as the obvious things that hit you immediately when you arrive, such as sights, sounds, smells and tastes, every culture has unspoken rules which affect the way people treat each other. The British generally have a reputation for punctuality. In business and academic life keeping to time is important. Arranging to meet to see a film at 8pm means arriving at 8pm. But if you are invited to visit someone's home for dinner at 8pm, you should probably aim to arrive at about ten minutes after eight. These subtle differences can be difficult to grasp.

Values

You may come to notice that people from other cultures may have very different views of the world from yours. Cultures are built on deeply-embedded sets of values, norms, assumptions and beliefs. As far as possible, try to suspend judgement until you understand how parts of a culture fit together into a coherent whole.

A MODEL OF CULTURE SHOCK

The process of culture shock can be illustrated by a model known as the 'W' curve (see diagram). This model may not relate to your experience or may do so only partially. Sometimes the process is faster or slower. Many people go through different phases of the process, so parts of the curve in the diagram may repeat themselves. The process can be broken down into five stages:

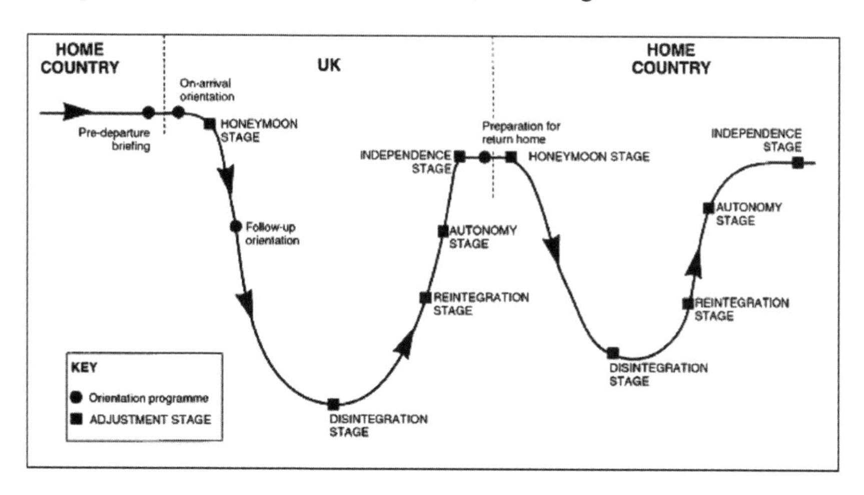

Adapted from *Orientated for Success*, edited by M Barker, Australian International Development Assistance Bureau, 1990.

1. The 'honeymoon' stage

When you first arrive in a new culture, differences are intriguing and you may feel excited, stimulated and curious. At this stage you are still protected by the close memory of your home culture.

2. The 'distress' or 'disintegration' stage

A little later, differences create an impact and you may feel confused, isolated or inadequate as cultural differences intrude and familiar supports (e.g. family or friends) are not immediately available.

3. 'Re-integration' stage

Next you may reject the differences you encounter. You may feel angry or frustrated, or hostile to the new culture. At this stage you may be conscious mainly of how much you dislike it compared to home. Don't worry, as this is quite a healthy reaction. You are reconnecting with what you value about yourself and your own culture.

4. 'Autonomy' stage

Differences and similarities are accepted. You may feel relaxed, confident, more like an old hand as you become more familiar with situations and feel well able to cope with new situations based on your growing experience.

5. 'Independence' stage

Differences and similarities are valued and important. You may feel full of potential and able to trust yourself in all kinds of situations. Most situations become enjoyable and you are able to make choices according to your preferences and values.

EFFECTS OF CULTURE SHOCK

- You may find your health is affected and you may get headaches or stomachaches.
- You may find it difficult to concentrate.
- You may become more irritable or tearful.

HOW TO HELP YOURSELF

- Simply understand that this is a normal experience – this may in itself be helpful.
- Keep in touch with home by telephone, letter, fax, email.
- Don't go home too often, as this will make settling more difficult.
- Have familiar things around you that have personal meaning, such as photographs or ornaments.
- Find a supplier of familiar food if you can.
- Eat a healthy and balanced diet.
- Take regular exercise
- Make friends with people in a similar position, as they will understand what you're feeling.
- Find some one to talk to who will listen uncritically and with understanding, rather than isolating yourself.
- Students should make use of the services offered by their college including counselling, group activities and social events.

Culture shock is entirely normal, usually unavoidable and not a sign that you have made a mistake or that you won't manage. In fact there are very positive aspects of culture shock. The experience can be a significant learning experience, making you more aware of aspects of your own culture as well as the new culture you have entered.

Useful contacts

TELEPHONE SERVICES

100 Operator (for help with calls locally, nationally and to the Republic of Ireland)

155 International Operator (for help with international calls or calls to a ship)

118 500 Directory Enquiries, British Telecom (can supply phone numbers for individuals and businesses in Britain if given name and location)

118 505 International Directory Enquiries (as above but for overseas individuals/businesses)

999 Emergency Services (police, fire, ambulance)

150 British Telecom (BT) customer services www.bt.com

Some special phone codes worth knowing include:
Toll-free: **0500/0800**
Local call rate applies: **0845**
National call rate applies: **0870**

EMBASSIES AND HIGH COMMISSIONS

Each country has an overseas representative based in the UK. Here are some of the most popular:

- American Embassy Tel: 020 7499 9000 www.usembassy.org.uk/
- Australian High Commission Tel: 020 7379 4334 www.australia.org.uk

- Bangladeshi High Commission Tel: 020 7584 0081 www.bangladeshhighcommission.org.uk/
- Brazilian Embassy Tel: 020 7499 0877 www.brazil.org.uk/
- Canadian High Commission Tel: 020 7258 6600 General Enquiries www.dfait-maeci.gc.ca/canadaeuropa/united_kingdom/
- Embassy of Chile Tel: 020 7580 6392 email embachile@embachile.co.uk
- Embassy of China Tel: 020 7299 4049 www.chinese-embassy.org.uk
- Indian High Commission Tel: 020 7836 8484 www.hcilondon.net/
- Indonesian Embassy Tel: 020 7499 7661 www.indonesianembassy.org.uk/
- Japanese Embassy Tel: 020 7465 6500 www.uk.emb-japan.go.jp/
- Embassy of Kenya Tel: 020 7636 2371/5
- Embassy of North Korea Tel: 020 8992 4965
- South Korean Embassy Tel: 020 7227 5500/2 http://korea.embassyhomepage.com/
- Malaysian Embassy Tel: 020 7235 8033
- Mexican Embassy Tel: 020 7499 8586 www.embamex.co.uk
- Embassy of Nepal Tel: 020 7229 1594/6231 www.nepembassy.org.uk/
- New Zealand High Commission Tel: 020 7930 8422 www.nzembassy.com/
- Embassy of Pakistan Tel: 020 7664 9200 www.pakmission-uk.gov.pk
- Embassy of Singapore Tel: 020 7235 8315 www.mfa.gov.sg/london/
- South African Embassy Tel: 020 7451 7299 www.southafricahouse.com/
- Sri Lankan Embassy Tel: 020 7262 1841 www.slhclondon.org/

- Thai Embassy Tel: 020 7589 2944 www.thaiinuk.com
- United Arab Emirates Embassy Tel: 020 7581 1281
- Embassy of Venezuela Tel: 020 7584 4206/7 www.venezlon.co.uk/
- Embassy of Vietnam Tel: 020 7937 1912

INDEPENDENT VISA ADVICE

www.amblercollins.com

GOVERNMENT DEPARTMENTS

www.ukvisas.gov.uk Government department site for UK visas.

www.dfes.gov.uk/providersregister.

www.hmce.gov.uk HM Customs and Excise provides advice on importing goods into the UK.

www.ind.homeoffice.gov.uk The immigration and nationality section of the Home Office is designed to help you understand the UK's immigration rules.

www.workpermits.gov.uk Work Permits (UK) administers the work permit arrangements for the UK government.

http://www.hmrc.gov.uk/ Features news and information relating to taxation and National Insurance in the UK.

www.dwp.gov.uk/lifeevent/benefits/ni_number.asp Provides information relating to how to obtain a National Insurance number, about pensions, benefits and services.

www.nhs.uk Set up over 50 years ago, the National Health Service is the largest provider of free health services in Europe.

NHS Direct Helpline (England, Wales and Northern Ireland) 0845 46 47 telephone-based service of the NHS.

NHS Direct Helpline (Scotland) 0800 22 44 88.

FOR INTERNATIONAL STUDENTS

www.ukcosa.org.uk Advice for international students

www.educationuk.org British Council site listing courses in the UK and lots more
www.fccollege.co.uk.

OTHER USEFUL CONTACT DETAILS

Postal services www.royalmail.com 08457 740 740 Find an address or postcode, track a parcel and get postal prices for all types of UK and international post.
Directory Enquiries 118 118 or 118 888.
Speaking Clock 123.
British Association for Counselling and Psychotherapy 0870 443 5252.
Relate (relationship and sexual counselling/issues) 0845 130 4016.
Alcoholics Anonymous 0845 769 7555.
National Missing Persons Helpline 0500 700 700 www.missingpersons.org

BANKS

The main retail banks in the UK:

www.barclays.co.uk
www.lloydstsb.co.uk
www.hsbc.co.uk
www.natwest.co.uk.

MAPS

www.streetmap.co.uk Enter a street name or postcode and this online service will bring up the relevant map.

BRITISH TOURIST AUTHORITY

www.visitbritain.com Provides details of all the interesting and beautiful places to visit in the UK.

EDUCATION IN THE UK

www.britishcouncil.org Information on UK education; can offer individual advice to those wanting to find a UK-based study course.

TRANSPORT

National Rail	0845 748 4950
Eurostar	01233 617 575
Eurotunnel	0870 535 3535
London Gatwick Airport	0870 000 2468
London Heathrow Airport	0870 000 0123
London Luton Airport	01582 40 5100
London Stansted Airport	0870 000 0303
Virgin Trains	0845 722 2333
London Underground	020 7222 1234
Docklands Light Railway Hotline	020 7918 4000

Index